A Promise of Justice

A Promise of Justice

David Protess

and

Rob Warden

New York

 Printed in the United States of America. For information address Hyperion, 114 Fifth Avenue, New York, New York 10011.

Library of Congress Cataloging-in-Publication Data

Protess, David.
A promise of justice/by David Protess and Rob Warden.
p. cm.
Includes bibliographical references.
ISBN 0–7868–6294–7 (alk. paper)
1. Murder—Illinois—Chicago—Case studies. 2. Afro-American prisoners—Illinois—Case studies. 3. Judicial error—Illinois—Case studies. I. Warden, Rob. II. Title.
HV6534.C4P76 1998
364.15'23'0977311—dc21 97–36431
CIP

Designed by Helene Wald Berinsky

FIRST EDITION

10 9 8 7 6 5 4 3 2 1

In Memory
of
Sister Miriam Wilson, O.S.B.

CONTENTS

Injustice anywhere is a threat
to justice everywhere.

—Martin Luther King, Jr.

■ ■ ■

Get out of the way of Justice.
She is blind.

—Stanislaw Jerzy Lec

A Promise of Justice

1

Dead Men Flying

TUESDAY, MAY 16, 1995

As a fleeting stillness settled over the Condemned Unit of the Illinois State Penitentiary at Menard, the occupant of cell 103, thirty-eight-year-old Dennis Williams, drifted off to sleep and into a recurring dream.

The dream was his favorite, one he'd first had seventeen years ago this very week. Williams, known to his keepers as A63823 and to his friends as Buck, was floating, weightless, high above the prison, his arms outstretched, his eyes on the traffic below.

He was soaring over Interstate 57, which traversed Illinois from the Mississippi River, where the medieval-looking prison rested on a limestone cliff, to East Chicago Heights in south suburban Cook County, which was once his home. Watching the cars head north, he felt euphoric, completely removed from captive life.

Suddenly, he was drawn to a car below, a sleek sedan with a velvet interior. He slid behind the wheel and started the engine. But when he hit the accelerator, hoping finally to head home, the car stalled, and the scene faded. If only he could *finish* the dream.

In the darkness, he awoke to thunder and lightning. He was alone, in a six-by-ten cell, lying on a thin mattress over a hard metal frame. Between thunderclaps, there was a barely audible noise, the whirring of a distant helicopter.

It had come for his closest friend, thirty-seven-year-old Girvies Davis, N06107, known to his friends as Preacherman. The chopper would fly Preacherman to the Stateville Correctional Center at Joliet, where executions were performed.

A full day would pass before Buck would learn Preacherman's fate. The governor could grant clemency, or Preacherman would die by lethal injection. But Buck was optimistic.

Just before Preacherman had been moved to isolation in preparation for the trip to Stateville, Buck had sent him a kite—a letter passed hand-to-hand, cell-to-cell along the tier, the Death Row equivalent of interoffice mail.

"I have faith that the governor is going to grant your clemency petition," said the kite. "You have very solid grounds of evidence and strong support from a mass of people, white and black. There's never been this much opposition around the death penalty since it's been in existence." The kite closed, "See you in the yard tomorrow."

As dawn approached, Buck lapsed into fitful slumber, awakening an hour or so later to a warm spring day—a hopeful sign, he thought. Perhaps Preacherman would be spared the fate the state had decreed for both of them in 1979, when judges at opposite ends of the state sentenced them to die for murders they swore they hadn't committed.

■ ■ ■

While the chopper beat its path north by northeast to Joliet, a red Mustang convertible raced up Sheridan Road toward the Evanston campus of Northwestern University. Its driver, David Protess, was laying on the horn, darting through early rush-hour traffic.

Protess was on a desperate mission, a last-ditch effort to save Girvies Davis's life. His strategy at this point, after five months of gumshoeing and crusading, was simply to turn up the heat on Illinois Governor Jim Edgar.

A crew from WGN-TV, the Chicago superstation, was camped on the front lawn of Fisk Hall, home of Northwestern's Medill School of Journalism, where the forty-nine-year-old Protess was a professor. He was to appear live, along with Ryan Owens, a sandy-haired Medill senior who was twenty-two years old—the age Girvies Davis had been when he was sentenced to die.

Owens was one of ten students who'd worked on Davis's case as a class project designed to give aspiring journalists real-world investigative experience. All eleven, students and professor, had gradually come to believe that Davis had been wrongly condemned. And they were intent on derailing his death.

By now, the sound bites were well-honed, which was fortunate because Protess and Owens would have only three minutes at 7:06 this morning to state the case for clemency before WGN's coast-to-coast audience.

While the case had looked bad at first—Davis stood convicted of four murders—the Northwestern investigative team had cast considerable doubt on the evidence.

In the sole murder for which Davis was facing death, that of eighty-nine-year-old Charles Biebel, there was no physical evidence linking him to the crime. No witness at the trial had placed Davis at the scene. Davis, an African-American, had been convicted of the Biebel murder by an all-white jury almost solely on the basis of a written confession, which Davis had signed at a time when he was illiterate.

But the kicker was that, while in police custody, he'd signed similar confessions to virtually every major unsolved crime in a two-county area—including three murders the authorities later acknowledged he couldn't have committed.

Davis claimed the confessions had been extracted at gunpoint, on the shoulder of a deserted road, in the middle of the night. Indeed, police logs showed that shortly before midnight officers had taken him for a "drive-around for evidence," after which, at 4:30 A.M., he'd signed the confessions.

After Protess and Owens summarized those facts, WGN reporter Larry Potash asked why the courts hadn't recognized the injustice.

"Because they didn't hear all the evidence," Protess answered. "It's a case of poor man's justice. Girvies had a court-appointed lawyer who didn't adequately represent him at the trial. The courts didn't even hear that he was illiterate."

When the interview ended, Protess invited Owens to his cluttered office to plan strategy for the rest of the day. As they talked over coffee and bagels, the phone rang. The caller identified himself as Tommie Page and said he'd just seen Protess and Owens on television.

In a voice filled with emotion, Page explained that he'd been a Davis juror in 1979. "We never would have found him guilty if we'd known he couldn't read or write," said Page. "Is it too late to do anything?"

At Protess's suggestion, Page agreed to fax the governor a plea for Davis's life. The message, transmitted at 9:31 A.M., less than fifteen hours before the scheduled execution, said Davis's illiteracy would "have made a big difference" to jurors. Their deliberations had been rushed, Page wrote, because "I had to take a final exam that night [and] no one wanted to be sequestered."

The fax concluded, "I believe my verdict was wrong. I deeply regret this terrible mistake on our part, and I hope it does not cause [*sic*] Mr. Davis his life."

As Owens excitedly called the other students to report the development, Protess did interviews about the juror's recantation with Chicago's two all-news radio stations. A reporter with WBBM News Radio contacted the governor's press secretary, Mike Lawrence, who confirmed that Page's fax had been received.

The governor would review it, along with more than a thousand other faxes and e-mail messages received in recent days pleading for Davis's life, Lawrence said. He added that an announcement of the governor's decision, scheduled for late morning, had been postponed several hours.

Protess and Owens exchanged high-fives. While neither public opinion nor a juror's recantation would be important in a court of law, they might be just what was needed to persuade Edgar to exercise his discretionary power to commute a death sentence.

Protess asked Owens to call the other students back and invite them to his home that evening for what he hoped would be a victory celebration.

■ ■ ■

In contrast to the optimism in Evanston, the mood was somber at One IBM Plaza in Chicago, home of the silk-stocking law firm of Jenner & Block. For a decade, a crack team of Jenner lawyers led by Notre Dame graduate Russell Hoover had been fighting *pro bono* for Girvies Davis's life. At every turn, they had been thwarted.

Just the day before, the U.S. Supreme Court had issued a terse order refusing to intervene in the case. A week earlier in the state capital, the Illinois Prisoner Review Board had sat stone-faced as Hoover and company presented an impassioned case for clemency. Their witnesses, including Protess and Owens, had been badly outnumbered by victims' family members and police officers who wanted Davis dead.

The board had made a secret, non-binding recommendation to the governor. Regardless of what the recommendation had been, the lawyers saw little cause for optimism because the Republican governor had made his support of the death penalty the cornerstone of his reelection campaign just six months earlier.

Since the election, the governor had allowed the state to proceed with its first double execution in forty years—an event that claimed the life of Hernando Williams, a client of another Jenner partner, Barry Levenstam. Like both Girvies Davis and Dennis Williams, Hernando was an African-American condemned by an all-white jury for an interracial crime.

Still reeling from Hernando's death, Levenstam had thrown himself full-time into the Davis case, willing to confront enormous odds for the cause.

Also recently joining Russ Hoover on the case were three young Jenner associates. One of them, David Schwartz, fresh out of the University of Michigan Law School, had taken on the extracurricular activity of establishing a Girvies Davis home page on the World Wide Web. It was the first use of the Internet to build public support for a condemned prisoner.

Schwartz, who'd grown especially close to his client, was appalled by the specter of the execution. He knew Davis as a gentle soul, a model prisoner, a transformed man.

Born to a prostitute in an East St. Louis slum, Davis was a fourth-grade dropout. He'd learned to read and write on Death Row—under the tutelage of Dennis Williams—and earned a high school equivalency degree. Eventually ordained as a minister by Grace Bible College, Davis was never seen without his tattered Bible. He'd become the Preacherman of Death Row.

Even Schwartz often found himself leaning on Davis for moral support, as he did when Davis called shortly before noon from his isolation cell near the death chamber at Stateville. "Don't worry about me," Davis calmly counseled. "I'm at peace."

▪ ▪ ▪

Rob Warden was at his desk at the Cook County State's Attorney's Office in Chicago's Loop practicing heresy—doing everything he could think of to encourage the governor to stop the execution.

Warden, a fifty-four-year-old former legal affairs writer and avowed opponent of the death penalty, had championed Dennis Williams's cause for thirteen years. At Williams's urging, Warden had persuaded Protess to join him in tackling the Girvies Davis case.

In the eighties, Warden had been the editor and publisher of *Chicago Lawyer*, a monthly magazine that specialized in exposing miscarriages of justice. He'd brought Protess on as a contributing editor in 1986, five years after Protess began teaching at Northwestern.

They were a study in contrasts. Warden, reared in southwest Missouri, was cautious and precise. Protess, a native of Brooklyn, was brash and impulsive. While Warden relished plowing through arcane legal documents, Protess specialized in getting reluctant sources to talk.

But, steeped in the culture of the sixties, they shared a deep mistrust of authority and a passion for muckraking. Collaborating on exposés of wrongful convictions and law enforcement improprieties, they'd earned reputations as congenital do-gooders among friends and foes alike, the latter including countless prosecutors.

In 1989, *Chicago Lawyer* was struggling financially and Warden reluctantly sold it. He then seized an opportunity to help elect Jack O'Malley, a reform-minded, politically ambitious young lawyer, as state's attorney of Cook County.

Despite Warden's infamy among frontline prosecutors, O'Malley hired him as executive officer. Warden became the office's ambassador to Chicago's public-interest community and, in exchange, his views were heard on policies and cases about which he felt passionately.

Warden had been planning an internal lobbying offensive on the Dennis Williams case when the Illinois Supreme Court set the execution date for Girvies Davis.

After Williams implored him to help Davis first, Warden organized a Girvies Davis Clemency Committee of prominent attorneys, academics, religious leaders, and former law enforcement officials. The committee put out more than 100,000 copies of a four-page brochure summarizing the findings of the Northwestern investigation.

In the week before Davis's scheduled execution, the committee sponsored a series of widely covered press conferences. At one, former Chicago Police Superintendent Richard J. Brzeczek, an ardent supporter of capital punishment, proclaimed, "This is the kind of case that gives the death penalty a bad name."

Now, with only a few hours to go, Warden enlisted the help of Andy Knott, the state's attorney's press secretary. Knott called his friend and counterpart in the governor's office, Mike Lawrence, to say that granting clemency wouldn't be unpopular in Cook County—even in law enforcement circles.

Anxiously pacing, Warden jumped for the telephone each time it rang. Around 3:00 P.M., Protess called.

"Any idea what's going on?" he asked.

"Not a goddamn clue," Warden said.

Protess had just heard from Davis. "He's a lot calmer than we are," Protess reported. "All he wanted to talk about was his helicopter ride this morning—said it was fun."

"Let's hope it wasn't his last one," Warden responded.

Warden said he would be leaving shortly to join a candlelight vigil at Stateville, but Protess prevailed upon him to join the gathering with the students instead. "Whatever happens," said Protess, "we should all be together tonight."

■ ■ ■

At 4:55 P.M., Joan Protess had just put lasagna into the oven and was headed upstairs to watch the TV news with her husband when the phone rang. Protess took the call out of the earshot of Joan, a Chicago attorney, and their ten-year-old son, Benji, a Davis pen pal who'd written the governor pleading for clemency.

It was a producer from WBBM News Radio. "Do you have a comment on the governor's decision?"

Protess took a deep breath. "What did he decide?"

"He denied clemency," she answered matter-of-factly. "The execution's going forward."

Stunned, Protess paused. "I'll have to call you back after I tell my wife and son," he said softly.

"But I need a reaction for the top of the news," she persisted.

Protess slammed down the receiver and raced to the TV room, shouting, "Turn the set off!"

"Oh, no," said Joan. Benji, realizing the news was bad, burst into tears.

After a few minutes, Protess turned the TV back on, just in time to catch channel 7 reporter Andy Shaw quoting Edgar's prepared statement: "The courts have had ample opportunity to fully review all of the arguments raised by Davis's supporters and rejected them. I am convinced that he is responsible for the murder for which he received the death penalty."

The students, watching the news at Ryan Owens's apartment before joining their professor, were outraged. Contacted for comment, they issued a statement calling the governor's decision "an act of personal and political cowardice."

They asserted that Jim Edgar lied in claiming the courts had considered all the arguments, when no court ever had taken Davis's illiteracy into account. "We have been taught in our journalism classes that the facts are paramount," the statement continued, "but apparently that was not enough to save Girvies Davis."

The students, who'd grown close to each other and to Davis as they repeatedly crisscrossed the state in his service, now made one final trip together for the death watch.

■ ■ ■

As the students arrived at David Protess's home, a hard rain had begun to fall, and there were reports of tornadoes and thunderstorms in the East St. Louis area, where Girvies Davis had been convicted.

Musing about the symbolism of the weather, the group picked at the lasagna and promptly downed the students' contribution to the occasion—a fifth of J&B scotch, Protess's favorite.

Around 9:00 P.M., Protess received two calls in rapid succession.

The first was from Barry Levenstam, who said he'd just filed a final appeal with the Illinois Supreme Court citing the juror's recantation and a statement the students had obtained from a prisoner attesting to Davis's illiteracy at the time he'd signed the confessions. "It doesn't have a prayer," said Levenstam, "but at least it will drag a judge out of bed to deny it."

The second call came collect from Stateville. Girvies Davis was on the line, calling to say good-bye. Protess put him on the speakerphone, and the group gathered around. "Try not to mourn for me," Davis said. "Move on with your lives. Just try to help people like me who get caught up in the system." He called the students "winners," telling them he deeply appreciated their efforts.

"We'll never forget you," Ryan Owens said.

Davis had a final request: He wanted Protess and the students to promise that this wouldn't be their last crusade in a capital case.

The room fell silent. "Of all the guys you know on the Row, who do you think most deserves help?" Protess asked.

"Buck Williams," Davis answered without hesitation. "I'm certain he's innocent."

Protess, who was familiar with the case from his *Chicago Lawyer* days, vowed that he and his next group of students would leave no stone unturned for Williams.

"And I promise *you* that, when my earthly being is gone, you'll have my spiritual presence to guide you," Davis said. "I'm gonna haunt you."

After a pause, he added, "I love you, brother."

■ ■ ■

When Rob Warden arrived shortly after 9:00 P.M., Protess related the promise he'd made to the doomed man—a promise Protess was far from sure he could keep.

"After this, Rob, I don't think I'm up to it," he said.

"But we can't quit now," Warden said, with more bravado than conviction.

On this night, the thought of another failure seemed too much for either to bear.

WEDNESDAY, MAY 17, 1995

At six foot four, *Chicago Tribune* columnist Eric Zorn stood head and shoulders over the crowd of reporters gathered under the tent on the well-manicured lawn of the Stateville Correctional Center.

An unabashed liberal in the conservative bastion that was the *Tribune*, the thirty-seven-year-old journalist had begun looking at Girvies Davis's case in the dead of winter at the urging of David Protess and Rob Warden.

Zorn had taken up Davis's cause in eleven columns, branding the prospective execution "obscene." Now he awaited the official word that it was over.

It came at 12:28 A.M., when the Department of Corrections spokesman, Nic Howell, appeared before a bevy of cameras and microphones to report that the execution had been "routine." Davis, Howell said, had declined a last meal. His final words had been, "I wish Godspeed to all."

St. Clair County State's Attorney Donald Haida, who'd witnessed the execution, said Davis's death had been "very peaceful compared with the violent death of his victims."

"Do you think it should have been worse?" Zorn asked.

"I believe in humane executions," Haida responded.

Reporters shouted predictable questions, which drew predictable answers. Enough, Zorn thought. He headed home, where he'd left a note for his wife to read to Davis if he called.

Davis indeed had called, at 9:50 P.M., and Johanna Zorn shared the message: "Your story has called attention to some very important and troubling aspects of capital punishment. I hope that people will remember them so that your death will not be in vain."

Davis left word in response: "We got the victory."

"I considered it a comforting rationalization, a skinny silver lining," Zorn ended his column the next day. "I didn't really think of the execution as a victory until I [learned] that Girvies Davis had proclaimed it so."

■ ■ ■

The news did not arrive at Death Row until morning.

Dennis Williams took it hard.

He'd deluded himself into believing there was hope for his best friend, and hope for himself. But the criminal justice system—more criminal than just in his mind—had murdered Preacherman and, with one round of appeals left, his own death was near.

Williams's thoughts turned to three childhood companions with whom he'd maintained a distant but powerful bond for seventeen years.

There was Verneal "Lurch" Jimerson, devout, quiet, now residing on Death Row at Pontiac, in the north central part of the state.

There was Willie "Tuna" Rainge, romantic, fun-loving, now serving a life sentence at Stateville, where Preacherman died.

And there was Kenny Adams—who'd somehow escaped a street moniker—charismatic, iron-willed, now languishing in some godforsaken dungeon unknown to Buck.

They'd stayed out of trouble on the mean streets of the poorest suburb in America, until the morning of May 12, 1978, when two white people turned up dead in their neighborhood.

The rest was history. Lurch, Tuna, and Kenny were Buck's rappies, codefendants in the legal vernacular, who'd rather rot than rat to save themselves.

They'd maintained their innocence, like Buck, unwaveringly but to no avail. And they were telling the truth, Buck knew—not only because they were incapable of violence, but because he was with them shortly before those white people were killed. They couldn't have been involved, no more than he could have.

They'd been done in by the white power structure, he was convinced: white cops, white prosecutors, white judges, white jurors. A few brothers—their lawyers and a neighbor—had sold them out, as had one sister—a girlfriend. But the real problem was power-tripping racists.

Some white do-gooders had helped, even getting him and Tuna new trials. But they'd ended up back behind bars. Now some of the same do-gooders had failed Preacherman.

Buck turned up the volume on the reggae playing on his handmade eight-track stereo system. Bob Marley was singing "Exodus." Ordinarily a comfort, the music couldn't drown his rage.

Buck would never ride home in that gray sedan. It had only been a dream.

His next trip out of Menard would surely be by helicopter.

2

A Letter from Death Row

WEDNESDAY, SEPTEMBER 16, 1981

A tattered manila envelope bearing the return address "Condemned Unit, Box 711, Menard, Illinois" arrived at the South State Street office of *Chicago Lawyer* among bills, subscription payments, and junk mail.

Curious, Margaret Roberts opened it. Though she'd seen more than her share of prison mail since Rob Warden hired her as managing editor the previous year, this letter was different. It was the first she'd read from Death Row.

"I hope it would not be too forward of me to ask your mercy and heart in an injustice I have suffered," it began. The writer claimed that he and some friends had been convicted of a rape and double murder three years earlier "based on perjured testimony."

He implored *Chicago Lawyer* to print his version of the facts. "I am not taking your magazine for granted," he wrote, "but I wish you could help me."

The letter closed, "Veritably yours, Dennis Williams."

Roberts showed the letter to Warden, who glanced at it over his usual breakfast of an Egg McMuffin and coffee. He remembered the news coverage of this case, which certainly made the defendants out to be guilty.

"Do you think it's worth checking out?" she asked.

"No harm in taking a look at the testimony he claims is perjured," said Warden, who was preoccupied with another story. "It wouldn't be the first time the media got it wrong."

Roberts returned to her office, thinking of all the other things she had to do. In addition to her long hours at *Chicago Lawyer*, she was supposed to be working on her doctoral dissertation in English literature at the University of Chicago.

She could assign the story to one of *Chicago Lawyer*'s two staff reporters, but they were consumed with other work. Letter in hand, she eyed her empty trash bin.

On impulse, she tacked the letter to her bulletin board.

■ ■ ■

Two weeks later, Margaret Roberts found yellowing copies of the trial transcript in a musty storage room at the Richard J. Daley Center, the rusty steel edifice that housed the Illinois Appellate Court.

As a fall chill descended on Chicago, Roberts immersed herself in details of the case that had landed Dennis Williams on Death Row.

The crime had been horrific.

■ ■ ■

Sometime after 2:30 A.M. on May 11, 1978, a Clark filling station in the mostly white suburb of Homewood was looted and the overnight attendant and his fiancée kidnapped.

The young couple, Larry Lionberg and Carol Schmal, had just become secretly engaged. It was Larry's first night on the job, and Carol was keeping him company.

They were taken to an abandoned townhouse in the black community of East Chicago Heights, about a fifteen-minute car ride away.

Larry's body was found at mid-morning on May 12 by two brothers, ages eight and eleven, who were playing on the bank of Deer Creek, a couple of hundred feet from the townhouse. He'd been shot twice in the head and once in the back with a .38-caliber pistol.

About forty-five minutes later, Carol's body, naked from the waist down, was discovered by police in a second-floor bedroom of the townhouse. She'd been raped and shot twice in the head with the same gun that had killed Larry.

■ ■ ■

From a snapshot in the court file, Margaret Roberts was struck by how much Carol Schmal resembled her.

Both were tall, slender brunettes with brown eyes and high cheekbones. Carol was twenty-three years old, about the age Roberts had been when the crime was committed.

Larry appeared in the same photo, which was taken on his twenty-ninth birthday, less than a month before the crime. He had shoulder-length hair and a beard. His broad smile was that of a young man in love.

■ ■ ■

Carol Schmal was the second of three children born to George and Joann Schmal.

Growing up in the North Roseland community on Chicago's southwest side, the Schmal children received a strict Catholic upbringing and attended parochial schools.

In the eighth grade, the nuns chose Carol as May Queen, an honor bestowed on the pupil who best exemplified the values of the Virgin Mary: purity, innocence, and compassion for others. In a school ceremony, Carol wore a white gown and a crown of flowers, which she took from her head and placed on the head of a statue of Mary.

In 1973, the family moved to a one-story brick bungalow in south suburban Glenwood, where Carol shared a bedroom with her older sister, Lynn. Carol was gregarious but reflective, spending much of her spare time reading poetry and philosophy.

After graduating from Our Mother of Sorrows High School, where she'd been a class officer, Carol majored in physical therapy at Northern Illinois University. She transferred briefly to the University of Idaho in 1977, but soon became homesick. Returning to her family, she took a job at a south suburban mental health center, where she helped women through late-night emotional crises.

Over the Christmas holidays that year, Carol told family members about her budding relationship with Larry Lionberg. She called him her "soul mate" and spoke of marriage.

On May 11, 1978, Carol was expected at the third birthday party of her godson Jeffrey, Lynn's oldest child. Lynn was worried when Carol didn't show up—it wasn't an event Carol would miss. After the party, Lynn received a call from a friend who'd heard on the radio that Carol was missing and that foul play was suspected.

The next day, George Schmal identified his daughter's body, and then broke the news to his wife, who was in the hospital with a back injury. Special arrangements had to be made for Joann Schmal to attend Carol's wake, on Mother's Day.

■ ■ ■

For most of Larry's childhood, the Lionberg family lived in Lansing and Dolton, Illinois, working-class southern suburbs.

The second of four children, Larry attended public schools and graduated from Thornridge High in 1967.

He worked at odd jobs and moved into a rooming house in a high-crime area of the racially mixed community of Harvey. His greatest fear, he told family members, was that he would be shot to death.

An extremely shy, gawky youth, Larry had no serious girlfriend before Carol. He loved motorcycles and playing cards with friends, including the rooming house owner's sons, who introduced him to Carol in the fall of 1977.

It was love at first sight, and the pretty, outgoing Carol brought out the best in him. He took his first full-time job, working for a security agency. When he was laid off because of cutbacks, he soon found employment at a Clark filling station in Harvey. He scrimped and saved for an engagement ring, which he and Carol picked out on May 10, 1978.

The same day, the manager of another Clark station, a few miles to the south on Halsted Street in Homewood, needed someone to fill in on the night shift. Larry's supervisor recommended him, and, eager to pick up a few extra bucks, he took the job. Because he didn't own a car, Carol drove him to work that night in her 1972 Chevy Malibu.

On May 12, William Lionberg identified his son's body at the county morgue.

■ ■ ■

The Cook County Sheriff's Police took charge of the multi-jurisdictional investigation, the abduction having occurred in one suburb and the murders in another.

Margaret Roberts noted that the first break in the case came at 12:50 P.M. on May 12, when the sheriff's police received an anonymous call from a man who claimed the killers were among a crowd "watching the police work on the bodies." The caller said the killers drove "a red Toyota and an orange Chevy." He added that he might come forward if they were caught.

When officers at the scene were notified of the call, they approached the crowd. Two young black men "bolted," looking over their shoulders as they walked "briskly" toward a red Toyota. The men, Dennis Williams and Verneal Jimerson, were taken into custody on the spot. The Toyota, which was Williams's, was impounded.

A few hours later, the sheriff's police questioned two of the suspects' friends, Kenny Adams and Willie Rainge. Adams admitted spending time with Williams the night of the crime, and Rainge owned a Chevy Vega the police believed was the second car described by the anonymous caller.

The next morning, May 13, Charles McCraney, a thirty-six-year-old self-styled jazz guitarist and composer, appeared at the sheriff's police office. McCraney, who lived across a courtyard from the abandoned townhouse where Carol's body had been found, identified himself as the anonymous caller and offered to testify if he could be relocated for protection.

McCraney said that in the wee hours of May 11 he was playing a guitar serenade he'd composed when he was interrupted by a commotion outside. Peering from a window, he saw a group of people and the two cars he'd described in the anonymous call.

A man got out of the red Toyota and broke a streetlight with a stone, according to McCraney. A few minutes later, the Toyota became stuck in mud near the abandoned townhouse. After the group freed the car, McCraney saw "six to eight people" run into the townhouse at "about 3:00 to 3:15 A.M." Then, he heard a single gunshot.

While McCraney had no clock, he fixed the time the group ran into the townhouse in relation to a late-night detective show he'd watched on television before playing his serenade.

From police photographs, McCraney identified three members of the group—Dennis Williams, Kenny Adams, and Willie Rainge—as men he'd often seen in the neighborhood. He did not claim to have seen Verneal Jimerson and, in the darkness, he could not discern the race or gender of the others.

On the morning of May 12, McCraney joined the crowd that had gathered at the murder scene, where he said he overheard Williams "jokingly" ask another man, "Did you shoot *those people*?" before the second body had been found.

Finally, McCraney told the police there might be another important witness, a young woman who lived a couple of doors from him. He'd seen her with Williams, Adams, and Rainge shortly before they ran into the abandoned townhouse.

Her name was Paula Gray.

■ ■ ■

Margaret Roberts had never seen a witness quite like Paula Gray. If Gray's initial statements were to be believed, Williams and the others were guilty. If her later statements were true, they likely were innocent.

Paula, the seventeen-year-old girlfriend of Kenny Adams, had been questioned repeatedly by police and prosecutors beginning on May 13, shortly after Charles McCraney mentioned her.

On May 16, she testified before a Cook County grand jury that she'd witnessed the rape and murders. She said she'd held a "Bic-type" cigarette lighter, providing the only illumination inside the pitch-black townhouse, while Schmal was raped seven times by four men—Williams, Adams, Rainge, and Jimerson.

After the half-hour gang rape, Paula testified, Williams shot Carol twice in the head. Larry was marched to the bank of Deer Creek, where he was shot twice in the head by Williams and once in the back by Rainge. Then Williams threw the gun into the creek.

Paula's statements sealed the case for prosecutors, who charged all four men with murder, rape, aggravated kidnapping, and armed robbery.

A month after the men were charged, however, Paula dramatically changed her story. At a pretrial hearing, she declared her four friends innocent and claimed police and prosecutors had forced her to lie. She testified: "I didn't hear nothing. I don't know nothing. I ain't saying nothing."

Prosecutors responded to the recantation by charging Paula with perjury and, believing her first statement, with murder and most of the other charges lodged against the men.

But the prosecutors were forced to drop the case against Verneal Jimerson, since Paula's statement had been the sole evidence against him.

Jimerson was a free man—for the time being.

■ ■ ■

The remaining male defendants had maintained their innocence with a vehemence that Margaret Roberts found compelling.

The state's case was bolstered, however, when a twenty-five-year-old East Chicago Heights man claimed to have heard Dennis Williams and Willie Rainge make some damning admissions. David Jackson had been in the Cook County Jail on a burglary charge when he said he overheard them talking about "a shot of pussy [they] really shouldn't have took from the lady."

According to Jackson, Williams said he was glad they "took care of the guy" and reassured Rainge, "They'll never find the pistol, you know."

■ ■ ■

Four months after the crime, Paula Gray and the three men went on trial before Judge Dwight McKay in the Cook County Circuit Court's south suburban branch, renowned for law-and-order judges and gung-ho prosecutors.

In an unusual move, McKay impaneled two juries, one for the men, one for Paula. When evidence admissible against Paula but not against the men was presented, the men's jury was excused, and vice versa.

Only Paula's jury heard about her conflicting statements, which the law prohibited from being used against the men. Only the men's jury heard the testimony of David Jackson, the jailhouse snitch.

But both juries heard most of the evidence, including testimony from family members of the victims. Larry's father, William Lionberg, testified he'd last seen his son alive on his birthday and next saw him on a metal slab at the county morgue. Carol's sister Lynn testified she'd last seen Carol alive a few days before the murder, and next saw her in a casket at the Mother's Day wake.

Margaret Roberts realized the testimony had been allowed to establish that the victims were once alive and were now dead—a legal requirement in a murder case—but she could only imagine the powerful impact it must have had on the juries.

Both juries heard testimony establishing that the abduction had occurred between 2:30 and 3:00 A.M. A friend of the slain couple testified that she and her boyfriend had visited them at the Clark station until 2:15, and an investigator testified that Larry's former employer had spoken to him on the phone at 2:30 A.M. Then, at 3:00 A.M., the sheriff's police had logged, but hadn't acted on, a call from a man who'd reported that the station was unattended.

The prosecution relied on Charles McCraney to place the defendants at the murder scene after the abduction. He identified each of the four in open court, saying he'd seen them together the night of the crime. McCraney told both juries that the three male defendants and others had run into the abandoned townhouse between 3:00 and 3:15 A.M.

The remainder of the prosecution's case included an array of forensic scientists, evidence technicians, and law enforcement officers involved in the investigation.

The most significant of these, Roberts thought, was Michael Podlecki, a criminalist with the Illinois State Police, who'd tested blood and hair evidence in the case.

Podlecki testified that he'd analyzed several Caucasian head hairs recovered from the trunk and backseat of Williams's car. Three of the hairs, he'd concluded, "matched" the hair of Carol Schmal and Larry Lionberg.

In addition, Podlecki said, at least one of the rapists had been a "type A secretor"—a blood group shared by about 25 percent of the population. Both Williams and Adams, he said, were A secretors.

Other officials provided details about the bloody crime scene and identified photos of the victims' bullet-ridden bodies.

The crime scene evidence, Roberts observed, virtually matched the original testimony of Paula Gray.

■ ■ ■

Focusing on the defense case, Margaret Roberts was astounded that Dennis Williams and Willie Rainge had been represented by the same lawyer who represented Paula Gray.

This seemed to be a rather blatant conflict of interest because Gray's grand jury testimony had led to the charges against the men—and because she could always flip again. But no one seemed to mind, and the trial had proceeded.

The lawyer, Archie B. Weston, and his three clients were joined at the defense table by James F. Creswell and his sole client, Kenny Adams.

The lawyers presented two lines of defense: alibi testimony and the lack of physical evidence linking their clients to the crime.

Unfortunately for the defendants, their alibis placed three of them together on the night of the crime and near the very spot where McCraney said he'd seen them. Paula Gray, Dennis Williams, and Kenny Adams indisputably were hanging out in front of the Gray house, but they said this was two or three hours before the time McCraney claimed they were there.

Gray testified that Williams and Adams had left shortly after midnight and she'd gone to bed. The mothers of all of the men swore they'd been at home well before 3:00 A.M., and Willie Rainge and his girlfriend testified they'd been together the entire evening.

Williams took the stand and denied both that he'd broken the streetlight and that his car had been stuck in the mud. Of dozens of crime scene photos, Roberts noted, there was none showing either a broken streetlight or a rut where a car might have been stuck. And the photos of the red Toyota showed no mud on its tires.

Through cross-examination, the defense established that no fingerprints or bloodstains linked the defendants to the crime. Nor was any of the loot taken from the Clark station—money, cartons of cigarettes, soda pop, and distinctive brown leather vests—found in the possession of the defendants. Finally, despite an exhaustive search of the area of Deer Creek where Paula had said Dennis Williams had thrown the gun, the murder weapon was never recovered.

The defense lawyers argued in closing that the evidence was insufficient to prove the defendants guilty beyond a reasonable doubt.

But to Roberts the defense seemed shaky: alibi statements by mothers and girlfriends and a few holes that might be explained by the defendants covering their tracks.

Maybe good enough in a garden-variety crime, but not in an interracial gang rape and murder.

■ ■ ■

Guilty, *guilty*, *guilty*, *guilty*. The men's jury deliberated less than four hours and Paula Gray's just two.

On October 24, 1978, four days after the verdicts and twenty-six days after the first witness testified, prosecutors announced they would seek the death penalty for the men. They sought prison for Paula, who wasn't eligible for death because she'd been under eighteen at the time of the crime.

In sentencing hearings that stretched into the next year, the prosecutors emphasized the brutality of the crime while the defense introduced the backgrounds of the defendants in mitigation.

Margaret Roberts already knew how brutal the crime was, but

was surprised to learn more about the people found guilty of committing it. They just didn't seem the type.

All came from devoutly religious families. Paula Gray, Kenny Adams, and Willie Rainge had no criminal records, and Dennis Williams had been convicted only of a property crime when he was a teenager. Roberts thought it remarkable that they'd stayed so clean growing up in hardscrabble East Chicago Heights, where a criminal record was virtually synonymous with adolescence.

Kenny and Dennis were graduates of Bloom High School, and their teachers testified they were cooperative and considerate of others. Kenny had a steady work history as a maintenance worker at Sears, Roebuck and Company and at a south suburban hospital. Dennis, although unemployed at the time of his arrest, had recently completed an auto mechanics program in pursuit of a job. Willie had been working ten hours a day at a car lot, having dropped out of high school to help support his two children.

How, Roberts wondered, could such men suddenly have become armed robbers, kidnappers, rapists, and killers?

Then there was Paula, the enigma. Her trial testimony had seemed reasonably articulate to Roberts. However, intelligence test results introduced at her sentencing hearing indicated she was borderline mentally retarded, with an IQ between fifty-five and seventy-five.

While Paula had come across as a strong and confident witness before the grand jury, earlier psychological evaluations had characterized her as "timid," "insecure," and "unstable." Less than a week after her grand jury appearance, she'd been hospitalized with an "acute schizophrenic reaction."

Who was the real Paula Gray? And which of her stories was true?

Judge McKay seemed certain of the answers, which he stated at sentencing. In his opinion, Paula was "streetwise," and her "violence and cruelty" had drawn her willingly into the crime.

"In her own environment," he said, "she is aware and intelligent." He concluded, "I'm really convinced her conduct justifies an extended sentence."

Accordingly, he gave her fifty years in prison.

In Kenny Adams's case, the prosecutors belatedly withdrew their request for death because he, unlike Williams and Rainge, wasn't alleged to have been a shooter. But McKay concluded, "He was there when violence was being contemplated. As a high school graduate, he was knowledgeable that serious harm was a probability. By his inaction, he committed murder. By his silence, he participated."

On the same day McKay sentenced Paula, he handed Adams seventy-five years.

Sentencing Rainge and Williams was more complicated because they demanded a hearing before another jury. That jury's role was to determine whether their crimes made them candidates for the death penalty and, if so, whether any mitigating factors justified a lesser punishment.

The sentencing jury quickly found both men eligible for execution—no surprise to Roberts, since Illinois law authorized the death sentence for multiple murder and for any killing committed in the course of another felony.

After considering the mitigating evidence in Rainge's case, the jury couldn't unanimously agree on whether he deserved to die. It was left to McKay to impose a prison sentence, which he did: life without parole.

The jury found insufficient mitigation to spare the life of Williams, who prosecutors said had been the ringleader and had fired four of the five shots that killed the victims.

On February 6, 1979, before pronouncing sentence, McKay asked Williams if he had anything to say. Williams again professed his innocence, calling the case "a prefabricated lie" and accusing the prosecutors of encouraging witnesses to commit perjury.

Without responding, McKay asked, "Are you ready to be sentenced?"

"I really have no choice," said Williams.

"I now sentence you then, Mr. Dennis Williams, to death," said McKay.

McKay's words echoed in Roberts's head as she closed the last volume of the transcripts, pondering two lives snuffed out, four others wasted.

At sentencing, Gray had just turned eighteen, and Adams, Rainge, and Williams were only twenty-one.

Could anything—*should* anything—be done to save them?

■ ■ ■

The next morning, a bleary-eyed Margaret Roberts was sipping black coffee at Rob Warden's desk when he arrived.

"Hungover?" he asked.

"Worse," she said. "I've been up all night thinking about the Williams case."

For the next hour, she talked nonstop, glancing occasionally at the notes she'd made in a purple spiral notebook.

Warden was riveted.

When she finished, Warden asked what she thought.

"I'm not sure," Roberts said. "But Paula Gray's grand jury testimony seemed pretty persuasive. It's hard to imagine that she could have made up so much stuff that turned out to be accurate."

"Maybe she didn't make it up," Warden said. "Maybe somebody fed it to her." And, he noted, not everything Paula said made sense. "She couldn't hold a Bic lighter for half an hour. Those things get hot real fast."

Roberts suggested that perhaps she should try to interview Paula, who was at the Dwight Correctional Center, a two-hour drive from Chicago.

"I don't think that's the first step," said Warden. "Whatever she says wouldn't count for much. She's a convicted perjurer."

Warden was more intrigued by Charles McCraney, noting that there were only thirty to forty-five minutes between the time the victims were last seen alive and the time McCraney estimated he saw the people run into the townhouse.

"He didn't have a clock and he pegged the time to some TV show?" Warden asked. "What show was he watching?"

"*Kojak*," said Roberts. "He said after it was over, he played a forty-five-minute guitar serenade. He'd just started to play it again when he saw the people run into the townhouse."

"What time was *Kojak* over?"

"It's not in the court record. No one asked."

Warden said he would try to find out from program logs at channel 2, the local CBS station, which carried *Kojak*.

Meanwhile, Roberts would check out Archie Weston, the defense lawyer. And, despite her editor's admonition, she intended to see Paula Gray.

First, however, she would answer the letter tacked to her bulletin board. She would ask Dennis Williams to call collect with more information about the key players in the case, information that wasn't in the trial transcripts.

She would make no promises, still skeptical of his story and daunted by the prospect of taking on the criminal justice establishment in a capital case.

But her curiosity, and the challenge, drove her forward.

3

The Detective and the Dude

■ Rob Warden feigned a frown as he interrupted a meeting Margaret Roberts was having with *Chicago Lawyer*'s staff reporters in her cramped office.

"I got the stuff on *Kojak* from channel 2," he said.

After a long pause, Roberts asked, "Well, are you going to tell me?"

"Says here," he finally told her, breaking into a smile, "the show ended at 12:50 A.M."

Roberts quickly did the math.

"Christ," she exclaimed, "even if McCraney played his goddamn guitar serenade twice, it would have only been 2:20."

"Right," Warden said. "It looks like he puts the guys in the Heights when Larry and Carol were still alive and well in Homewood. If anything, his testimony should have helped the defense."

How, they wondered, could both of the defense lawyers, Archie Weston and James Creswell, have missed something so obvious?

■ ■ ■

Archie Weston was an outgoing and selfless man, willing to help those in need even if they couldn't afford his services, sources in the legal community told Margaret Roberts.

However, because many of Weston's clients were slow-pay or no-pay, several lawyers and judges expressed concern that he routinely took more cases than he could handle. He also devoted considerable time to bar association activities, serving as president of the National Bar Association, the organized black bar. By the time he represented Dennis Williams, Willie Rainge, and Paula Gray, he'd practiced law nineteen years, and his colleagues felt that he'd burned out.

Not surprisingly, Weston's performance during the trial had been challenged in 1980 by the court-appointed lawyers handling the defendants' appeals. The appellate briefs had cited a plethora of alleged errors and omissions. Among them, Roberts noted, were Weston's failure to effectively question witnesses, failure to object to the introduction of the hair evidence—the product of a warrantless search of Williams's car—and failure to make even the most routine motions, including one for a new trial after the verdicts.

Kenny Adams's appellate defenders hadn't made James Creswell's performance an issue, but they asserted that their client's case had been hopelessly prejudiced by Weston's bungling.

When Creswell was hired by Kenny Adams's family, he'd been practicing law twenty years in the south suburbs. He and a partner handled mostly real-estate closings, wills, and minor criminal cases. Adams was his first murder case.

A routine check of civil litigation records turned up nothing on Creswell, but Roberts discovered that Weston had a serious legal problem of his own—a problem that had come to a head at the very time he was defending Williams, Rainge, and Gray.

In 1978, Weston had been accused of mishandling the estate of an elderly woman. Just days after his three clients and Kenny Adams were convicted, he was removed as administrator of the estate and held in contempt of court for failing to appear.

Then a $23,000 judgment was entered against him. When he was unable to satisfy it, his home was seized and sold at a sheriff's auction.

To make matters worse, the Illinois Attorney Registration and Disciplinary Commission was investigating Weston and had subpoenaed his financial records. When he'd failed to comply, the agency initiated proceedings to determine whether Weston should be disbarred.

■ ■ ■

"Margaret Roberts?"

"Yes?"

"Will you accept the charges on a collect call from Dennis Williams?"

"Yes."

Williams's voice was deep and melodic. "Thank you for answering my letter," he said. "It's a pleasure to meet you, even if it's only on the phone."

"Maybe we can meet in person someday," she said. "For now I've got a bunch of questions to ask."

But Williams had an agenda of his own. Over the blare of boomboxes, clanging, and shouting, he launched into a soliloquy about his path to Death Row. He vented about those he blamed for his plight: Archie Weston ("a buffoon"), the police and prosecutors ("a legion of corruption"), the judge ("a third prosecutor"), Paula Gray ("scared and confused"), and Charles McCraney ("a scam-man").

Roberts realized it would be futile to interrupt with specific questions. She was annoyed at first, but soon found herself captivated by the power of his narrative. Williams was a strong-willed, articulate man of obvious intelligence. Roberts knew he'd never give up without a fight.

When a voice came on the line saying the call would be disconnected in one minute, Roberts managed to steer the conversation back to McCraney.

"His lies," said Williams, "were bought and paid for with reward money and other things."

"What reward money?" Roberts inquired, having seen no reference to it in the trial transcripts.

"Clark Oil Company put up two grand," he said. "McCraney got a piece of that, and he got thousands more from the state for moving expenses. He's supposed to be in some kind of witness-protection program."

"How do you know?"

"My kid brother hired a private investigator. He found it out after the trial."

Williams said the investigator, René Brown, was trying to track down McCraney.

And, Williams added, just before the phone went dead, Brown had developed a lead on the real killers.

■ ■ ■

René Brown was smooth. He talked smooth, walked smooth, and looked smooth.

When he appeared at the *Chicago Lawyer* offices a few days before Christmas of 1981, he sported a well-coiffed Afro and carried a bulging leather briefcase. Tinted, gold-framed glasses only partially obscured his intense eyes.

For a man in his late twenties, Brown had seen a lot. He'd been a defense investigator in more than a score of murder cases.

Brown had attained a measure of fame for shooting holes in the prosecution case against seventeen prisoners who'd faced the death penalty for killing three guards at the Pontiac Correctional Center. All seventeen had been acquitted.

The Pontiac case had brought Brown to the attention of Dennis Williams's appellate lawyers, who'd introduced him to Williams's brother, James.

"James Williams was certain his brother was innocent and wanted me to prove it," Brown told Margaret Roberts. "I was busy, but I took a look at some of the files."

Brown said it was the red Toyota that first grabbed his attention. "It was just this tiny, little car," he reflected. "How'd they fit all those people in there? It didn't make sense. I said to myself, 'I have to take this case.' "

James Williams, a Greyhound bus driver, and his wife, Vella, a legal secretary, had agreed to pay Brown as he went along. Willie Rainge's family also contributed financially, as well as in another important way.

Rainge's aunt, Virginia Hawkins, had introduced Brown to a man who seemed to know a lot about the crime. In fact, the man claimed to have firsthand information that Rainge and his codefendants were innocent. The man's name was Dennis Johnson, known around the Heights as "the Dude."

Hawkins, who knew Johnson because she'd dated his father, had accompanied Brown in August of 1980 to the Body Snatchers Lounge, a topless lounge in East Chicago Heights. There they'd met the younger Johnson, an ex-con whom Brown described as "a drug-pushing gangbanger."

Johnson agreed to talk with Brown—in private. Leaving Hawkins at the bar, they went into the men's room. "I know who did the murders and how the whole thing came down," Brown quoted Johnson as saying.

Johnson said he'd tell the whole story if Brown could guarantee him immunity from prosecution. Brown couldn't promise that, but he wanted to string Johnson along. "I'll see what I can do," he said, "but you'll need to tell me more."

After thinking it over, Johnson agreed to meet Brown and two of Dennis Williams's lawyers the next day at the home of James Williams in the middle-class Beverly neighborhood of Chicago.

■ ■ ■

Sitting at James Williams's dining room table, Johnson related that a couple of days after the murders he'd bought a .38-caliber revolver and a sheepskin vest from a man named Red. He'd paid $25 for the gun and $7 for the vest.

Later, Johnson mentioned the purchases to "a friend," who told him why the price of the gun was so low: It had been used to kill Larry Lionberg and Carol Schmal.

The friend, whom Johnson wouldn't identify, had been involved in the crime, along with Red and two other men. "We stuck up the Clark station," Johnson quoted the friend as saying. "We took the dude and broad to the Heights. They fucked the broad, but I didn't want any. Then they decided to take them out so they couldn't go to the police."

Johnson claimed that he'd confronted Red, who reluctantly confirmed the story. Red also told him that the car used in the crime had been a 1970 or '71 Buick Electra 225, known on the street as a "deuce and a quarter," and that its owner had been one of the killers.

Johnson would say no more in front of the lawyers, both of whom were white. When the lawyers left, however, Brown persuaded him to talk further, "brother to brother."

Admitting that the story he had just told was not entirely true, Johnson now explained why he needed immunity from prosecution: He'd been present for the gas station robbery and abduction.

"The plan was to stick up someplace to get money," he said, "but things got out of control."

After the abduction, Johnson said, he insisted that Red drop him off at a pool hall across from the Body Snatchers and urged him to let the couple go. He claimed he didn't see Red again until he'd sold him the gun and vest.

When Brown asked what Johnson had done with the gun, he said he'd "sold it to a dude from Minnesota." He offered to retrieve the gun, reveal Red's full name, and identify the owner of the deuce and a quarter—but only if Brown could deliver immunity from prosecution.

Even then, Johnson said, he would not name the fourth man involved in the crime, his "friend."

■ ■ ■

Margaret Roberts listened intently to René Brown's tale, which he told as if he were reliving it, pausing from time to time to light a Newport.

"So what do you think?" she asked Brown.

"I think there's something to it," said Brown, pointing out that Dennis Johnson had accurately described the murder weapon and one of the leather vests taken from the gas station. "And the big Buick Electra fits the facts a lot better than a little red Toyota."

"Interesting," Roberts said. "But why's Johnson talking to you?"

"I don't know his angle," Brown replied, "but he says he just wants to set it right. He hasn't asked for money or anything. Just immunity, or he won't go public with his story."

"Can I talk to him?" Roberts asked.

By now, Johnson was back in prison for armed robbery, Brown said, but they'd stayed in touch. He'd find out if Johnson would see Roberts.

"A gang-banging, drug-dealing, stick-up man," said Roberts. "Sounds real credible."

"Well, he's certainly the type who'd rob a gas station," Brown pointed out. "He's a helluva lot more likely suspect than the choirboys they convicted."

That opinion was shared, he added, by everyone he'd interviewed in East Chicago Heights, where he'd spent countless hours futilely searching for Charles McCraney and Red. ("Red," Brown explained, was a common nickname for black men with ruddy skin.)

The search ended when the Williams and Rainge families could no longer afford Brown's services, and he'd moved on to other cases. "But," he said, "this one still haunts me."

Roberts knew an invitation when she saw one—and she took the bait, agreeing to pay Brown to pick up where he'd left off.

Together, the detective and the journalist would continue the investigation behind prison walls and in the projects of East Chicago Heights.

■ ■ ■

The glory days of East Chicago Heights had passed long before Margaret Roberts and René Brown drove its streets. Once a way station on the underground railroad for slaves escaping to Canada, it had been a prosperous agricultural community through the first half of the twentieth century.

After World War I, hundreds of blacks from the South gravitated there as workers and sharecroppers on farms operated mostly by Polish, Lithuanian, and Italian immigrants. The community was 90 percent black by 1949, the year it was incorporated as a separate entity from primarily white Chicago Heights.

In 1956, Ford Motor Company opened a stamping plant on the eastern edge of Chicago Heights, offering blacks an equal opportunity for well-paying jobs and turning the East Heights into a reasonably prosperous blue-collar suburb.

But the town's fortunes took a turn for the worse in the mid-sixties, when the federal government subsidized housing projects to accommodate poor blacks displaced by the construction of a Chicago campus of the University of Illinois. The new single-family public housing—townhouses clustered around courtyards—also attracted other blacks from Chicago's crowded high-rise projects.

The population of East Chicago Heights doubled in little more than a decade, peaking at 5,300 in the mid-seventies. And with the influx of urban poor came crime and decay. Families soon began abandoning the deteriorating townhouses, including one at 1528 Cannon Lane, which became infamous in 1978.

The following year, a downturn in the world auto market forced Ford to lay off six hundred local workers—a disaster for the economy of East Chicago Heights.

By the time René Brown gave Margaret Roberts her first grand tour on a freezing January Sunday in 1982, East Chicago Heights had been declared by sociologist Pierre DeVise to be the poorest suburb in America.

■ ■ ■

Stray dogs roamed the streets. Drug dealers casually hawked their wares in front of a liquor store on Route 30, the road that ran past the East Chicago Heights Police Station. Abandoned houses dotted the landscape, stripped of their aluminum siding—a source of cash for a fix.

But Margaret Roberts and René Brown also saw signs of hope. Well-scrubbed children and parents in their Sunday best spilled from churches. The windows of the graffiti-free Medgar Evers Elementary School displayed cheerful drawings and posters announcing community meetings. And the smell of down-home cooking wafted from split-level homes on the southeast side of town.

It was at one such home that Roberts and Brown made their first stop. They were welcomed warmly by Claudette Adams, a petite, strikingly pretty woman. She was the mother of five children, four of whom were home for Sunday dinner.

The room of the fifth, her youngest child, Kenny, was kept just as he'd left it in 1978. Roberts, fixing on Kenny's high school graduation photo, was taken by his good looks: finely chiseled features, smooth complexion, and warm brown eyes.

Beside the photo on a shelf stood trophies commemorating his seasons as the starting center fielder of the varsity baseball team. A copy of *From Ghetto to Glory* by Hall of Fame pitcher Bob Gibson lay on the bedside table.

When Kenny was in the sixth grade, in 1969, the family—Claudette, her second husband Joe Hurley, and the kids—had moved into the comfortable frame home from a cramped apartment in Chicago.

They'd faithfully attended services at Trinity Church of God in Christ. ("Reverend Nelson's church," Claudette called it.) The children had succeeded in the public schools and stayed out of trouble. Kenny, she said, had never even gotten a traffic ticket before being accused of the horrible crimes she was sure he didn't commit.

Claudette's certainty of his innocence, she told Roberts and Brown, was based on more than a mother's belief in a good son. She'd seen him when he came home a little after midnight on the night in question. She'd noticed his hair, which he told her Paula Gray had just braided.

More important, in Roberts's mind, Claudette said Kenny had turned down a last-minute deal that would have ensured his freedom. All he had to do was testify that his friends committed the crime.

Claudette was proud of his refusal to cave in to the pressure, in spite of the consequence. "I raised my kids to tell the truth," she said.

Now Kenny's home was Menard, a six-hour drive from East Chicago Heights, making family visits difficult and infrequent. He stayed in touch by mail and phone, and Claudette prayed he'd soon receive a requested transfer to a prison nearer Chicago.

Meanwhile, family members were doing what they could to help. His eldest sister, Juanita, had collected more than a thousand signatures on petitions asking the governor to intervene in the case. Juanita also had sent letters to civil rights organizations and national television programs. But the only responses she'd received were form letters.

After a couple of hours with the family, Roberts and Brown reluctantly declined an invitation to stay for dinner, saying they had other stops to make.

As they prepared to leave, Brown asked if Claudette knew of a man called Red who might be viewed as a suspect in the crime.

"Oh, there's lots of Reds around here," she said. "A family right over on Congress, the Robinsons, have a son called Red."

But, she hastened to add, "Red Robinson's a clean boy, like my Kenny."

■ ■ ■

René Brown showed Margaret Roberts the murder scene and the now boarded-up townhouses where the Gray and McCraney families once lived.

He pointed out a building that had housed a maintenance office when he last visited the area a year or so earlier. There, he told Roberts, he'd met Walter Sally, who'd been the custodian of the complex when the murders occurred.

Sally had told Brown there was something fishy about Charles McCraney's story: The streetlight McCraney claimed had been broken the night of the crime actually had been broken days earlier. Sally himself had swept up the glass.

He also said he'd known McCraney and promised to help find him. But Brown had gotten wrapped up with Dennis Johnson, and Sally had since vanished.

Before returning to Chicago, Roberts and Brown stopped for gas at the Homewood Clark filling station. When they went inside to pay, Roberts noticed a bright yellow sticker prominently displayed on the counter. It bore the logo: Bic.

She wondered if it had been there when the sheriff's police were investigating the crime. Could that sticker, in some way, have been the genesis of Paula Gray's improbable claim about the source of light in the abandoned townhouse?

■ ■ ■

Twenty-one-year-old Paula Gray was in handcuffs when Margaret Roberts and René Brown interviewed her at the Dwight Correctional Center.

Roberts and Brown brought Louise Gray along in the hope that Paula would feel more comfortable in the presence of her mother. But Paula was in no mood to talk.

Her appeal had been denied, and she faced being behind bars until middle age. The handcuffs were required because she'd been put into isolation for refusing to perform a prison chore.

"Mama, they be wantin' me to do heavy liftin' like a man," said the slender, soft-featured Paula, who seemed even younger than she was. "I ain't no man, and I ain't gonna do it."

As Roberts and Brown gradually began asking questions, Paula continued to look at her mother, responding softly with yes or no answers.

But when Brown finally got to the key question, Paula looked him right in the eyes and responded emphatically: "We didn't kill them white people."

What had once caused her to say she'd witnessed the crime?

Paula lowered her head and didn't answer.

"Did the police hurt you?" Brown asked.

She shook her head no.

"Where'd you get the idea about the Bic?"

More silence.

Brown pressed no further.

Roberts put away her notebook and listened as mother and daughter passed the remaining time deep in conversation about family on the outside and Paula's travails on the inside.

A few days later, in a letter to Dennis Williams, Roberts said she'd seen "a determination like steel" in Paula's words.

"She was very angry about being handcuffed, but quietly angry, full of dignity, actually, is the way she struck me," Roberts wrote. "I was surprised, to tell you the truth, because she had been described as borderline mentally retarded, and to my observation anyway, she was a very intelligent, proud woman, full of dignity and suffering."

Referring to Paula's assertion of innocence, Roberts closed the letter: "I'll say what I felt—she was telling the truth."

■ ■ ■

Unlike Paula Gray, Dennis "the Dude" Johnson seemed right at home in prison.

When René Brown took Margaret Roberts to see him, Johnson was doing his second stint at the Pontiac Correctional Center for armed robbery.

His first had been for a 1973 stickup in which an accomplice had shot and killed a liquor store owner. Johnson had been paroled in 1977, the year before the murders of Larry Lionberg and Carol Schmal. Now he was back, serving six years for relieving a man of a wad of cash at gunpoint across the street from the Body Snatchers in 1981.

Twenty-seven years old, with a short mustache and goatee, Johnson proudly flew the Gangster Disciples' colors—a black and blue cap tilted to the right. The words SEX and A-SHAY were tattooed on his biceps, the latter referring to a branch of the gang he'd founded at Pontiac.

He placed one condition on the interview: that Roberts and Brown would not disclose his name without permission.

That agreed, he repeated the story he'd told Brown a year and a half earlier: He'd been present for the gas station robbery and abduction, but had been dropped off by Red before the rape and murders.

But, in retelling the tale, he offhandedly referred to the owner of the Buick Electra used in the crime as Johnny, a name he hadn't previously mentioned.

"Can you tell us any more about Johnny or Red?" Brown asked.

"Not unless I get immunity," Johnson said, "because if you find 'em, they could flip on me."

"How do we know this isn't a bunch of bullshit?" Roberts asked.

Johnson paused, eyeing her. "I'll put you on to the piece," he finally said.

He said the .38 used in the murders was in Minneapolis and provided a telephone number of a woman who might lead them to it. "But you didn't get that from me."

Roberts nodded. Though skeptical of Johnson, she was intrigued by the possibility of coming up with the gun. If ballistics tests proved it to be the murder weapon, that would make Johnson credible and perhaps force the authorities to reopen the investigation and give him immunity.

While not wanting to seem ungrateful, she couldn't help wondering aloud why Johnson was apparently trying to help.

"Listen, I've done some bad shit in my life," he said, "but I don't wanna see a brother die for a crime he didn't do."

Johnson stroked his goatee.

"You know what's really fucked up? We left prints all over. I never got it—why didn't the cops find 'em and bust our asses?"

4

Blind Justice

■ Over steaks and beer at Binyon's, a walnut-paneled German restaurant around the corner from *Chicago Lawyer*, Margaret Roberts and René Brown brought Rob Warden up to speed on the investigation. It was late January of 1982.

Based on the information they'd uncovered, Warden could envision doing a story that raised troubling questions about the convictions.

But Roberts and Brown wanted to wait. They believed they could solve the crime. And Roberts had a plan that required more than a green light from Warden. She wanted him involved.

While she and Brown chased the .38 and continued to canvass East Chicago Heights, Warden would cultivate sources in legal circles to figure out how the apparent injustice had occurred.

Warden didn't take much convincing. This was just the kind of story he'd dreamed of doing when he started *Chicago Lawyer* three years earlier.

■ ■ ■

"I was devastated when I lost Kenny Adams's case," James Creswell told Rob Warden the next day. "There's no doubt in my mind he's innocent."

Creswell said he was haunted by what his client had told him in rejecting the deal that would have set him free in exchange for testifying against the others: "My body would have been free, but I would have been a prisoner in my mind."

Even after the trial, Creswell added, Adams had scoffed when prosecutors offered him a reduced sentence if he'd testify against Dennis Williams and Willie Rainge at their death penalty hearing. "I felt guilty even conveying the offer," Creswell said.

Asked what had gone wrong in the case, Creswell put it succinctly: "Everything.

"Archie Weston, God bless him, was in way over his head with three clients," Creswell reflected. "He was screaming up and down that he wasn't ready for trial. So what does the judge do? He starts jury selection at what we thought was just going to be a routine hearing. He caught everybody off guard—except the prosecutors."

Creswell characterized the prosecutors, Scott Arthur and Clifford Johnson, as "cagey veterans who outmaneuvered us at every turn." They used peremptory challenges to knock all blacks off the men's jury and all but a couple off Paula's, he said, and then inflamed both juries' passions with emotional testimony that had nothing to do with guilt or innocence.

"That Scott Arthur is a piece of work," Creswell said, shivering slightly. He pulled out all the stops.

"But the bottom line is that the sheriff's police either botched the investigation or lied through their teeth."

They testified, for instance, that they hadn't dusted the Clark station for fingerprints, claiming it wouldn't have been productive because the station had been too heavily trafficked.

Creswell didn't buy that explanation, noting that the sheriff's crime scene manual required dusting for prints in such situations.

He speculated that they'd in fact lifted prints and then denied doing so because the prints didn't implicate the defendants, or perhaps implicated someone else.

Similarly, Charles McCraney testified he'd signed a typed statement "two or three days after the crime," even though the cops claimed he hadn't. Creswell suspected the cops had "deep-sixed" the statement upon discovering that it placed the defendants at the scene too early for the victims to have been there.

And, Creswell pointed out, the cops had interrogated Paula Gray for three days, but denied taking any notes. "That," he said, "simply defies logic.

"I'm not making any excuses for my performance. I was naive and didn't really see the light until after the trial," Creswell concluded. "But in hindsight, this case was a rush to judgment—and, with white victims and black clients, we didn't have much chance."

■ ■ ■

Rob Warden reached a decidedly defensive Archie Weston at the apartment where he and his family had moved after losing their home.

In their curt conversation, Weston said he saw nothing wrong with simultaneously representing three defendants in a capital case, and contended that his problems with the estate had not affected his performance at the trial.

"If you want to know what went wrong," he said, "talk to the cops, not to me."

■ ■ ■

His subordinates in the Sheriff's Department called Howard Vanick "Steelheels," but not to his face.

Lieutenant Vanick, law enforcement sources told Rob Warden, fostered a tough-guy image, strutting through the corridors of the

Homewood sheriff's station with metal taps on his spit-shined shoes. He was a tall, broad-shouldered man with rawboned features and slicked-back hair.

In 1978, at age thirty-six, Vanick was a fifteen-year veteran of the sheriff's police and had been commander of south suburban investigations for three years. The first officer to arrive in East Chicago Heights after Larry Lionberg's body was discovered, Vanick promptly took charge of the investigation.

Vanick was soon joined at the scene by P. J. Pastirik, a former undercover narc, and David Capelli, a rookie investigator.

When Carol Schmal's body was found, Vanick declared he wanted the crime solved—and solved fast.

Two hours later, Pastirik and Capelli arrested Dennis Williams and Verneal Jimerson after they'd allegedly "bolted" from the crowd that had gathered.

The very next day, during a lengthy interrogation, Paula Gray fingered Williams and Jimerson, as well as the two other suspects provided by Charles McCraney—Kenny Adams and Willie Rainge.

Then Howard Vanick asked Louise Gray if it would be okay to take her daughter to the murder scene to look for evidence.

"By all means," Vanick quoted Louise as responding.

Around midnight, Vanick walked Paula through the abandoned townhouse, where Carol Schmal's blood was still on the floor, and to the bank of Deer Creek, where Paula indicated the gun had been thrown.

Paula was then taken into "protective custody" and housed for two nights in Holiday Inns, where the questioning continued. At no point was she threatened, according to Vanick.

As divers began searching for the murder weapon, Vanick was openly skeptical that it would be found.

"A nigger never gets rid of a gun," he told the men under his command.

■ ■ ■

Based on his own experience, Dennis Williams said he had little trouble imagining what the police had done to extract Paula Gray's damning statements.

He, too, had been taken for a midnight ride to the murder scene, Williams told Rob Warden in one of his increasingly frequent collect calls from Death Row.

With his hands cuffed tightly behind his back, Williams said, he'd been ushered into the townhouse by a contingent of cops, including P. J. Pastirik and David Capelli.

"Get up those stairs, nigger," he was ordered.

A cop, standing over a pool of drying blood on the bedroom floor, shoved a photograph of Carol Schmal in Williams's face. "That's how I found out she was white," he recalled, "and I knew I was done for."

Pastirik threw Williams against the wall, put a gun to his temple, and threatened, "Nigger, if you don't tell us what happened in the next three seconds, I'm gonna splatter your damn brains on the wall like you did Carol's."

"I told you I don't know nothin'," Williams wailed.

"What you waitin' on, P.J.?" said a heavyset officer with a wart on his nose. "Give me the goddamn gun, I'll kill that son-of-a-bitch."

Grabbing the gun from Pastirik, he pulled the trigger. Williams heard a click. "You put in the wrong clip," the officer told Pastirik. "Give me the one with the bullets in it."

Williams, perspiring heavily, heard the cop slam another clip into the gun, and again felt it pressed hard against his head. "Nigger, I'm gonna kill you."

"You're gonna *have* to," Williams said. "I never died before and tonight's as good a time as any, but I'm not gonna tell you I did it."

At this point, according to Williams, Capelli and Pastirik intervened, wresting the weapon from the heavyset cop.

"No, no, man, don't do it," Pastirik yelled. "There's no use wastin' your career over this fuckin' nigger."

■ ■ ■

Verneal Jimerson's encounter with P. J. Pastirik and David Capelli wasn't as brutal, though it was just as unforgettable.

They were the cops who'd busted him.

But their account of the arrest was false, he told Margaret Roberts and René Brown, insisting that he and Dennis Williams hadn't bolted from the crowd as the officers approached.

Jimerson said he'd gone to his brother-in-law's house in East Chicago Heights on May 12 after a power failure shut down the car wash where he worked.

Hearing that some people had been killed in the projects, they drove over to check it out. Jimerson spotted Dennis Williams and, having left his sunglasses in Williams's car two nights before, asked if he could get them.

Williams gave him the keys, and Jimerson—by himself—trotted to the red Toyota. Pastirik and Capelli immediately threw him against the car and slapped handcuffs on him. Williams came running over after he saw what was happening to Jimerson. Then they cuffed Williams, too.

When Jimerson was released after Paula Gray's recantation, he'd rejoined his wife and three daughters and gone back to work at the car wash.

His life seemed to be going well for the time being. But he was taking it one day at a time, haunted by nightmares that Gray would change her story and once again implicate him.

■ ■ ■

There was a troubled tone in Margaret Roberts's voice when she called Rob Warden at home on a Sunday morning in mid-February. She said she had something to discuss with him and, at her suggestion, they met for brunch.

Roberts began by saying that, after five trips to East Chicago Heights, she and René Brown still had no leads on Red or Johnny. And their exhaustive search of state motor vehicle records had shown a dozen 1970 and '71 Buick Electra 225s registered to residents of the Heights, but none to anyone named Johnny.

Roberts said she also was frustrated by their failure to track down the gun. The woman who Dennis Johnson had said could find it had flatly refused to cooperate.

"Any ideas where to go next?" Warden asked.

"René wants to move to the Heights and work the case from down there," she said, adding that he would stay at the home of Willie Rainge's mother.

"No harm in trying it for a while," Warden said. "We could really use you on a couple of other stories right now anyway."

Roberts leaned back in her chair. "I've got to tell you something, Rob," she said. "I got a call last week from the editor of the *National Journal*. They want me to interview for an editing job."

Warden was stunned, but tried not to show it. "It's a terrific magazine," he said. "It would be a great opportunity." The job would put her in Washington, an exciting place to practice journalism and her hometown, where her father was a patent lawyer.

But Roberts was ambivalent. There was her loyalty to Warden and her commitment to the Williams case. Besides, she wasn't even sure she wanted to stay in journalism. She'd always planned to finish her Ph.D. and become an author or literary critic.

"Margaret," Warden told her, "you've got to at least go for the interview. Otherwise, you'll always second-guess yourself."

As she nodded, Warden looked away. He didn't want to lose her.

■ ■ ■

After a week of nightlife in the Heights, René Brown reported that Red, Johnny, and the Buick deuce and a quarter seemed to draw blanks from pool hall hustlers, Body Snatchers boozers, and street-corner junkies.

But when Brown casually dropped the Dude's name, the reaction was the same each time: fearful stares.

The week had not been wasted, however, Brown assured Rob Warden. Brown had found a guy, who knew a guy, who'd led Brown to Walter Sally, the maintenance man at the projects in 1978. Sally was willing to help unlock a closely guarded secret of the prosecution: the whereabouts of Charles McCraney.

McCraney, Sally said, had been relocated to St. Anne, Illinois, a rural community about seventy-five miles southeast of Chicago. McCraney had no street address, just a post office box, but Sally knew how to find him.

Excited by this lead, Warden mulled over the question of who should go with Sally to see McCraney. Warden told Brown he wanted a journalist along, either Margaret Roberts or himself.

But Roberts was unavailable. She'd been offered the *National Journal* job and was in D.C. pondering what to do. Her absence had left Warden with the task of putting the finishing touches on the next issue of *Chicago Lawyer*.

Warden had also become embroiled in a breaking story about how an innocent man might have been framed in yet another death penalty case—a case, Warden told Brown, that could have ramifications for the East Chicago Heights defendants and others.

Under the circumstances, Warden and Brown agreed, McCraney could wait.

■ ■ ■

On April 12, 1982, the capital murder case that had drawn Rob Warden's attention came to a dramatic conclusion.

Cook County Circuit Court Judge William Cousins exonerated an eighteen-year-old honor student, the son of a police officer, of murdering a little girl during a home invasion.

George Jones had been on trial for his life when a Chicago police detective disclosed that his department had hidden a report indicating that someone else committed the crime.

Under oath in Cousins's courtroom, police officials were forced to admit that they commonly kept two sets of reports on criminal investigations: one they turned over to defense lawyers, one they kept to themselves.

The secret reports were known as "street files."

Watching the black teenager walk free, Warden felt a mixture of elation and outrage.

His thoughts drifted to Dennis Williams.

If the Chicago Police maintained street files, the Cook County Sheriff's Police almost certainly did, too.

■ ■ ■

Four days after George Jones won his freedom, Rob Warden was working on the street files story when he was interrupted by Oliver Smith, a *Chicago Lawyer* editorial assistant.

"Here's today's Illinois Supreme Court decisions," Smith said, plopping a manila envelope on Warden's desk. Opening the envelope, Warden flipped through the opinions.

He froze when he saw the caption: "*People of the State of Illinois, Appellee, v. Dennis Williams, Appellant.*" And then: "Judgment affirmed."

The majority opinion, written by Justice Robert Underwood, summarily rejected Williams's claims that the evidence had been insufficient to prove him guilty, that the dual juries were improper, that the case had been forced to trial too hastily, and that the death penalty was unconstitutional.

Underwood focused on only one issue: the effectiveness of Williams's trial lawyer. While tacitly recognizing that Archie Weston's performance might have been below par, Underwood wrote that "a defendant is entitled to competent, not perfect, representation." He added, "[H]indsight often dictates that different strategy might have produced better results. However, such 'errors' in judgment do not establish incompetency."

The opinion concluded by rejecting the argument that Williams was entitled to a new trial because blacks had been "systematically excluded" from the jury. Since Archie Weston hadn't objected during jury selection, Underwood held, the issue had been waived.

Justice Seymour Simon wrote a stinging dissent, rebuking Judge Dwight McKay for starting the trial despite Weston's strenuous objection that he wasn't adequately prepared.

"[T]he way this case was railroaded to trial embarrassed the defendant in his defense and prejudiced his rights," Simon wrote. "To force a triple capital case as complex as this one to trial under such circumstances was an abuse of [judicial] discretion."

Simon also attacked the majority for applying too stringent a test of incompetence, saying: "If the court can safely reduce every attorney to the level of a novice, we may as well all take the novice; he's cheaper."

Williams was entitled to a new trial, Simon concluded—but he stood alone.

His brethren scheduled Dennis Williams's execution for November 17.

■ ■ ■

Rob Warden called Margaret Roberts in Washington with the news. She sobbed, the first time he'd ever heard her cry.

He assured her that the execution date would be delayed pending appeals to the federal courts. "It's not too late to save him," he said.

But her sobbing continued.

Finally, she told Warden she'd been putting off calling him. She'd accepted the *National Journal* job.

Now, however, she was having second thoughts. "I want to be there to help," she said.

"You can't let this case control your career," Warden said. "And you can still help. I'll fly you back and we'll write the story together when it's ready to go."

That suggestion seemed to console Roberts, who said she felt selfish thinking about her career in light of what had just happened to Dennis Williams.

"Have you heard from him yet?" she asked.

Warden hadn't, but hoped Williams would call after his lawyers gave him the news.

"Give him my number, but please don't tell him the real reason I'm here," she said. "For now, at least, I can try to be of some comfort."

■ ■ ■

There was no comforting Dennis Williams.

His appellate lawyers, Martin Carlson and Steven Clark, had prepared him all along for the worst.

But when Carlson broke the news to him over the phone, Williams became enraged and abruptly ended the conversation after hearing little more than the vote.

How could six justices have failed to see that the trial had been a mockery and that, at the very least, he deserved another shot at justice?

After a guard retrieved the phone that had been brought to his cell for the Carlson call, Williams lost control. Venting his rage to other prisoners on the gallery, he screamed that the justices were "a corrupt bunch of lowlifes."

"They deserve to die," he howled.

"Yeah, we gotta kill 'em all," shouted a cop killer.

"Like the St. Valentine's Day massacre," a serial killer yelled.

Williams reveled in the growing chorus, carried away in a fantasy about lining the men in black robes up against a wall and opening fire. The cops and prosecutors, too!

But his head soon spun with conflicting emotions. He unsteadily retreated from the bars and braced himself against the metal wash-basin attached to his toilet.

As the voices from the gallery slowly subsided, so did his fury, leaving him overcome by loneliness—and shame. He would not cast his lot with men who were worse than the justices.

For two weeks, he shunned the privilege of leaving his cell for ninety minutes of daily exercise in the yard, a fifteen-by-fifteen-foot concrete slab surrounded by walls topped with razor wire.

He draped a bedsheet over the bars of his cell and spoke to no one, not even his lawyers, his family, or the journalists who wanted to bring his case to public attention.

He found consolation only in the kites he received from Girvies Davis, the Preacherman, who quoted Scripture and implored him to come to Sunday services—something Williams had not done since his arrest.

It was not the religious messages in the kites, but rather the recurring salutation that eventually roused Williams from seclusion on a Sunday morning in early May.

"Dear Brother Buck," each had begun.

■ ■ ■

In handcuffs and shackles, Dennis Williams entered the church of the condemned, a dimly lit room that, except on the Sabbath, was used for recreation. Punching bags and barbells surrounded the metal chairs that were imported for worship.

After guards removed his chains, Williams slipped into a chair next to Girvies Davis, who warmly embraced him.

The Reverend Ira Banks, the Death Row Protestant chaplain, began by quoting Psalms: "The steps of a good man are ordered by the Lord: and he delighteth in his way. Though he fall, he shall not be utterly cast down: for the Lord upholdeth him with his hand."

Paraphrasing Romans, Banks said the Devil sometimes works his will through powerful people, but faith in God could heal the corrupt.

"Amen," Williams said softly.

But when Banks spoke of love and forgiveness, Williams's mind wandered. He hoped the sermon would end before the allotted hour expired so that he and Davis could talk, but Banks didn't oblige.

As the prisoners lined up to be shackled and returned to their cells, Davis put a firm hand on Williams's shoulder and said, "Hope you found some comfort here, Buckaroo."

"It's hard to believe in anything in this godforsaken place," sighed Williams.

"God has not forsaken you," Davis rejoined. "Evil people have."

Williams, who had by now read the supreme court opinion in his case, said he'd taken solace in Seymour Simon's dissent.

"There's other people in the free world that will help you—if you let them," Davis said.

Williams thought of the encouraging letters he'd received from Margaret Roberts and Rob Warden since the court ruling. Like Simon, they seemed well intentioned, but had accomplished nothing.

When Williams reached the front of the line, he turned to face Davis as a guard cuffed his hands behind his back.

"God helps them that helps themselves," Williams said in a mocking tone.

"Have faith," Davis told him, as another guard snapped a chain around Williams's waist and led him away.

"The truth shall make you free," Davis called after him.

■ ■ ■

Back in his cell on the top tier of the gallery, Dennis Williams took down his makeshift curtain and pulled a manual typewriter from under his bed.

"I cannot be overcome by letting hopelessness loom over me," he wrote to Margaret Roberts. "I will not surrender my life as the passive livestock does before slaughter.

"Although I'm frustrating myself with the vindictive insanity of the supreme court's decision, I will do whatever you suggest as far as your story is concerned."

With the letter, Williams enclosed a poem titled "Escape from Death," which he'd written in 1980:

As I lie here in squalor of damnation, kidnapped and hated,
My heart beats with a broken rhythm, and my blood runs cold.
In search for escape, I stare out at the tranquilly emerging dawn, my only hope, life, the setting sun.
In this reality I'm free, no longer the Living Dead.
I'm not the ultimate sufferer of this ugly and wrongful condemnation,
Afloat and beyond this wretched Earth, a benediction to transcend this ailing Civilization.
So, Oppressor, do as you are willed, but in this life Truth will be fulfilled.

5

MOVING MINDS

▪ On an overcast spring day, Rob Warden picked up Walter Sally for the hour-and-a-half trek to St. Anne, Illinois.

René Brown chose not to go along because he felt "ganging up" on the state's star witness might make him reluctant to talk.

During the drive, Warden and Sally chatted about the best way to approach Charles McCraney. Sally, an outgoing, well-spoken man in his late twenties, said McCraney was a mistrustful sort who might be belligerent. They agreed that Sally would go in first, try to warm him up, and perhaps persuade him to go to a restaurant to talk.

McCraney lived about five miles south of town, in a dilapidated frame house near the end of a winding dirt road. As Warden pulled into the muddy driveway, barking dogs surrounded the car. Sally bravely got out and approached the front door, the hounds sniffing at his blue jeans.

A tall, mottled-skinned man cracked the door and peered outside. After a moment's hesitation, he stepped onto the porch and shook Sally's hand. The two men conversed briefly, with McCraney suspiciously eyeing the white man in the car.

Sally then put his hand on McCraney's shoulder and steered him to the car. Both men climbed in, McCraney into the backseat.

"Would you like to grab something to eat?" Warden inquired after the introductions.

"Already ate," said McCraney. "We can talk here."

"So how do you like living in the country?"

"Better than that rat hole."

"Safer, I bet."

"More peaceful, too."

McCraney went on to say there'd been almost constant racket in the East Chicago Heights neighborhood where he, his wife, and three young daughters had lived in 1978.

"Them boys was always around the Gray house, drinkin' and gunnin' their engines," he said. "My little girls was always bein' woke up, and I couldn't compose my music."

Warden asked about the serenade he was playing the night of the murders.

"Serenade Nineteen-ninety," said McCraney, pridefully.

With a little prompting, he described how he'd watched *Kojak* and then played the forty-five-minute composition. He'd started playing it again when he heard "them folks makin' a commotion" and saw them run into the abandoned townhouse.

"How much time passed between the end of *Kojak* and the folks running into the building?" Warden asked.

"About an hour," McCraney said.

"Was that the most it could have been?"

"Maybe an hour and a quarter."

Warden then told him that *Kojak* had ended at 12:50 A.M. and that the abduction couldn't have occurred until at least 2:30 A.M., more than an hour and a half later.

McCraney scratched his head.

"Well," he said, "maybe them folks is innocent."

He added, "I never said I saw 'em kill anybody. I never even said I saw 'em with any white people."

As if realizing the import of what he'd just said, McCraney reached for the door handle. "I don't want no more trouble," he said.

"Trouble with who?" Warden asked.

"Dennis Williams an' them," said McCraney. "I don't want 'em comin' after me. They [the prosecutors] moved me once, an' they ain't gonna do it again."

"They moved you?" Warden said, feigning surprise.

"Yeah, but they didn't pay for everything," McCraney said defensively. "Just a couple of grand."

"And you got a thousand-dollar reward from Clark Oil?" Warden asked.

McCraney nodded, but he clearly didn't like the direction the conversation had taken. "Hey, I shouldn't be talkin' to you," he said.

With that, he got out of the car and slammed the door.

■ ■ ■

By the time Rob Warden returned to his office from St. Anne, he'd decided that the Dennis Williams story would be the cover of *Chicago Lawyer*'s July 1982 issue.

But before bringing Margaret Roberts back to help put the story together, he wanted to turn up the heat on Dennis Johnson.

Warden wrote Johnson a letter saying, "We can wait no longer to write our story about the case, and I feel it will be necessary to quote you. I'm sure you realize that the issue here is an innocent man's life. All deals are off unless you can deliver the evidence you promised to deliver." If Johnson didn't want his name to appear in print, the letter said, he would have to identify the killers and the person to whom he sold the .38.

A few days later, the Dude called with a threat of his own.

"If you use my name, I'll come up with the gun all right," Johnson said. "And I'll say I got it from Dennis Williams."

■ ■ ■

Resigned to quoting Dennis Johnson anonymously, Rob Warden shifted gears to tie up one last loose end: the status of Archie Weston's legal problems.

Warden discovered that, in the pending disbarment proceeding before the Illinois Supreme Court, Weston had finally answered the allegations surrounding his mishandling of the elderly woman's estate.

Weston contended, in an affidavit, that he'd been "laboring under extreme emotional stress" in 1978 when he'd failed to comply with the subpoena for his financial records. He added that the loss of his home had caused him "untold worry and anxiety."

Now that the matter had reached the supreme court, Warden wondered if the justices would be forced to acknowledge a connection between Weston's performance at the trial and the turmoil in his life at the time.

■ ■ ■

While Rob Warden was bringing Dennis Williams up to date on developments in the investigation, he was interrupted by a call from, of all people, Justice Seymour Simon.

Warden had known Simon since 1966, when Warden was a reporter for the *Chicago Daily News* and Simon was president of the Cook County Board of Commissioners. *Chicago Lawyer* had endorsed Simon for the supreme court in 1980, in part because of his progressive stance on criminal justice issues, dating from his days as a Justice Department lawyer during the New Deal.

Simon was calling because he'd received an invitation to participate in a forum cosponsored by *Chicago Lawyer*. He planned to attend but wanted more information.

After Warden filled him in, Simon casually asked if he was working on anything interesting.

Warden mentioned the Dennis Williams case and, to Warden's surprise, Simon asked if they could get together, though he didn't say why.

That evening, Warden met the silver-haired, angular-faced jurist at the City Tavern, a Loop restaurant popular among lawyers.

Over drinks, Simon bemoaned his fellow justices' recent rulings on the constitutionality of the death penalty.

In 1979, the year before Simon's election, the court had upheld the Illinois capital punishment law by only a four-to-three vote. Death penalty opponents rejoiced that Simon's election had shifted the balance in favor of overturning the statute.

But the jubilation was premature. In 1981, the three justices who'd been in the minority changed their positions, saying they were bound by *stare decisis*, the precedent set by the previous majority.

That rationale, both men knew, was hogwash. The real reason for the change seemed obvious: The most notorious mass murderer in Illinois history had been convicted in the interim. And the elected justices feared the political consequences of voiding the law under which John Wayne Gacy faced execution for murdering thirty-two young boys.

When Warden tried to turn the conversation to the evidence suggesting that Dennis Williams might be innocent, Simon stopped him. "I can't talk about the facts of the case," he said. "It's not over."

"So what do you want to know?" Warden asked, puzzled about why Simon had wanted to meet.

"The lawyer in that case was a guy named Archie Weston, right?" Simon asked.

"Yes."

"How much do you know about him?"

"Quite a bit."

"Well, tell me this: Is he the same Archie Weston who's facing disbarment now?"

Seeing that Warden seemed a little taken aback by the question, Simon explained that the lawyer at the Williams trial was Archie Weston, Sr. but the one involved in the disbarment proceedings was Archie Benjamin Weston.

"I interviewed him on the phone," Warden said. "We talked about both cases, and there's no question he's the same guy."

"Well," said Simon, "this guy told us at his disbarment hearing last week that he was so hard up and under so much stress back in seventy-eight that he couldn't think straight."

"That's even stronger than his affidavit," Warden noted.

Simon nodded and changed the subject, obviously not wanting to discuss what he'd do next.

Resisting the temptation to pry, Warden just hoped the other justices shared Simon's continuing concern about the case.

■ ■ ■

During a long weekend in late June, Margaret Roberts and Rob Warden sat side by side at computer terminals, taking cracks at different approaches to the story.

René Brown hovered nearby, verifying facts and culling quotes from the massive files he'd assembled.

The floor was soon littered with discarded drafts, empty pizza cartons, and crushed pop cans that had missed overflowing wastebaskets.

After three days of writing and rewriting, interrupted only by occasional catnaps and arguments over wording, the final draft was ready—slightly past the printer's deadline, as usual.

"*Will we execute an innocent man?*" blared the cover headline. Inside, the headline was repeated above a photo of Dennis Williams, his hair in a tall Afro and his arms folded defiantly.

The snapshot of Larry Lionberg and Carol Schmal taken at Larry's last birthday party also accompanied the 8,000-word article.

The story began by highlighting the holes in the state's case and quickly turned to a detailed discussion of Archie Weston's legal problems.

It quoted Charles McCraney's statements about the timing of events and the money he'd received, followed by Dennis Johnson's anonymous rendition of the crime. (Johnson was described as "a man who says he could identify the actual perpetrators and is reasonably certain he could lead authorities to physical evidence corroborating his story," if he received immunity.)

Police photos of Kenny Adams, Willie Rainge, Paula Gray, and the murder scene were interspersed with a recounting of the shaky trial evidence.

The article closed with three paragraphs on the state supreme court's majority opinion and two on Seymour Simon's dissent.

July's issue of *Chicago Lawyer* had a press run of 22,000 that would circulate among attorneys, journalists, educators, and court buffs. But for this particular issue, Warden and Roberts had an even more select audience in mind: the justices of the Illinois Supreme Court.

■ ■ ■

Willie Rainge happened to be watching the channel 2 news in his cell at Stateville when his ex-lawyer's face flashed across the screen.

Rainge turned up the volume. "Archie Weston represented three of the codefendants," reporter I. J. Hudson was saying, "and reporters from *Chicago Lawyer* charge that Weston was rushed to trial and that he didn't provide an adequate defense."

The camera cut to Rob Warden saying it was "virtually unheard of" for one lawyer to represent defendants with conflicting interests.

"Two of the defendants might have gotten off if they had simply agreed to testify against Dennis Williams," Warden said.

Hudson resumed, "At the time of the trial Weston was being sued for allegedly mishandling an estate, but says his problems had no bearing on his handling of the Williams case."

The story also featured an on-camera interview with Williams—shackled in the prison warden's office—criticizing Weston for failing to conduct even a cursory investigation of the case.

It ended with Assistant State's Attorney Scott Arthur defending his trial adversary. Weston, the prosecutor contended, had "left no stone unturned" for his clients.

Rainge, elated by the TV report, called Warden the next morning and asked for a copy of the article.

Warden found Rainge's soft, engaging telephone manner surprising. They'd never spoken before, and Warden had imagined that his voice would match the steely scowl of his mug shot.

Rainge said he felt upbeat for the first time since the supreme court decision in the Williams case three months earlier. "When I heard how Buck's case came down, I figured the rest of us was stayin' put," said Rainge, whose own case was still pending before the Illinois Appellate Court.

Warden took the opportunity to learn more about Rainge's life behind bars.

Rainge lamented that his girlfriend, Patricia Hatten, who'd been his alibi for the night of the murders, had broken off their relationship soon after his conviction.

His children had visited him infrequently since his incarceration, and that was the way he wanted it. "Prison's no place to see 'em," he said, "but I miss 'em awful bad."

Arealya, his daughter, had been a fixture in the courtroom during the trial. The three-year-old once brought the proceedings to a halt by racing to the defense table, shouting, "Let my daddy come home, he ain't hurt nobody!" The judge ordered her returned to the spectator section, but Arealya scrambled around the table, temporarily eluding bailiffs.

Tederol, his son, had been an infant at the time of the trial. "You know," Rainge reflected, "I'd just changed his diaper and was headin' to work the day the cops took me in."

Rainge was worried about his children growing up in East Chicago Heights, which he'd once himself dreamed of escaping.

His mother, Georgia Beamon, and favorite aunt, Virginia Hawkins (who'd introduced René Brown to Dennis Johnson), also remained in the Heights and steadfastly supported Rainge. "But other kin has moved on, and I don't hear from 'em much," he said. "We was all so tight 'til this happened."

In maximum security, Rainge confided, he'd found a new family—the Black Disciples gang. Both his need for belonging and fear for his safety had led him to "affiliate."

"Ya know what can happen to a guy my size in here if he don't have protection," said Rainge, who stood five-nine and weighed a mere 125 pounds. "The Two-Fours will watch my back 'til I'm free."

"Two-Fours?"

"Yeah, B, D—two, four."

On a related matter, Warden asked how Rainge had come to be known as "Tuna," which sounded sinister to Warden, as in mob boss Tony "Big Tuna" Accardo.

Rainge laughed, explaining that, as a child, he had an unusual fondness for tuna fish. "My granddaddy gave me the name, and it just stuck."

Now, as a Two-Four at Stateville, he was known as "Sir Tuna."

■ ■ ■

Dennis Williams was riding high in the wake of the *Chicago Lawyer* story and his channel 2 interview.

On July 6, he wrote Margaret Roberts thanking her "for the work and cogency you put in the article for me."

He added, "I was really nervous during the channel 2 interview because the warden refused to leave the office." But he thought the interview "would have a positive impact on some people out there" and lead to other media opportunities.

"Having me filmed in chains, handcuffs, and leg irons was nothing short of an effort by prison officials to project me as some wild animal not to be trusted around civilized civilians," he wrote. "Looking at it another way, though, the shackles worked to my benefit: Here's an innocent man chained like a dog when he shouldn't be in prison in the first place."

Turning to the disclosures about Archie Weston, Williams said he was hardly surprised. "Weston suffers from an ailment common among lawyers," Williams wrote. "I have always perceived a vast percentage of them to be incompetent, overambitious, pseudo make-believers."

The question, as Williams saw it, was what impact the new information would have on six very important lawyers—the supreme court justices who'd set his execution date.

Williams was cynically optimistic: "The majority, afraid that these disclosures on Weston's profession may cast a bad cloud over their own heads, finds themselves almost compelled to renege on their decision. It's not the incompetence of Weston that they care about. It's their reputation.

"Whatever happens for the better or worse, I guess I'll just wait and see."

■ ■ ■

Thanksgiving of 1982 arrived a week early for Dennis Williams. The Illinois Supreme Court granted him a new trial on November 18, twelve days after it summarily disbarred Archie Weston.

The opinion, written by Robert Underwood, was unanimous—and Rob Warden instinctively knew that Seymour Simon was behind it.

The sole basis for the reversal was "the newly acquired information concerning Williams's counsel, which we have concluded may well have had an effect on counsel's ability to represent his client."

Underwood wrote, "We are now aware, for the first time, of the unique circumstances under which counsel in this case was operating at the time of the capital trial."

While Archie Weston's performance was not "of such a low caliber as to reduce the trial to a farce or sham," Underwood wrote, "we can no longer say with any degree of assurance that Williams received the effective assistance of counsel guaranteed by the Constitution."

Nevertheless, the opinion said that "although the evidence is in large part circumstantial, it does tend toward a satisfactory conclusion and produces a reasonable and moral certainty that the defendant committed the murders and rape."

It concluded, "We believe, however, considering the unique circumstances in this case, which will rarely, if ever, be duplicated, that the interests of justice require that Williams be granted a new trial."

After reading the opinion, without really pondering its uncertain implications, Warden excitedly placed a call to Washington.

When Margaret Roberts's machine answered, he left a simple message: "Congratulations. You just saved a life."

6

Reversals of Fortune

▪ It was like dominoes falling, Rob Warden thought, as Willie Rainge and then Paula Gray won new trials based on the Illinois Supreme Court's reasoning in the Dennis Williams case.

The legal system seemed headed toward a just result.

If prosecutors decided to retry the cases, Charles McCraney's testimony could be easily impeached. Gray, who had professed her innocence for five years, was unlikely to flip now that she'd won a major victory. And new defense lawyers, who'd surely be better than their predecessors, could discredit the rest of the state's case—shaky scientific evidence and a jailhouse snitch.

There also was still a chance Dennis Johnson would come up with the murder weapon and force the prosecutors to pursue the alternative suspects.

The bad news was that the Dude hadn't responded to repeated letters from Warden and René Brown asking him for more leads.

And Kenny Adams's appeal had been denied at the same time Willie Rainge's case was reversed. It seemed terribly ironic that justice might elude Adams simply because he hadn't been represented by Archie Weston. But Adams had plenty of appeals left, and he wasn't the type to give up.

All in all, the situation looked good, and so the case moved to the back burner for Rob Warden and René Brown.

Dennis Williams, however, was not so optimistic. The prosecutors had appealed his victory to the U.S. Supreme Court, putting his bid for freedom on hold. Rainge and Gray also were going nowhere until the top court ruled.

Williams expressed his discontent to Margaret Roberts in long letters and phone calls.

He lamented the growing conservative mood of the country and Ronald Reagan's "ascendency to the throne." Abhorring the administration's efforts to turn the federal judiciary to the right and expedite executions, Williams asked rhetorically, "I wonder who's worse today, Russia or the United States?"

His frustration became acute when his twenty-seventh birthday—his sixth on Death Row—passed on February 13, 1984, more than a year after the Illinois Supreme Court had reversed his case.

Roberts tried to console him. She reminded him of all he'd accomplished through sheer force of will and encouraged him to continue writing poetry and to pursue a newfound interest: electronics.

In one call, Williams had told her about a boombox he'd built with parts from old radios and a tape player discarded by other prisoners. He held it to the phone, filling her ears with the Queen of Soul, Aretha Franklin. Trouble was, Williams joked, the device was somewhat outdated: It only played eight-track tapes.

Roberts regretted there was little she could do on the case, although she did write Paula Gray's mother in the hope of bolstering Paula's resolve. Roberts invited the Grays to call collect, but wasn't overly concerned when they didn't respond. She'd been infected by Warden's optimism that the legal system was on the right track.

And, finally, their faith was rewarded when the U.S. Supreme Court, on May 19, 1984, let the Illinois decision stand.

The defendants now appeared to be in a win-win situation. The state could either drop the charges or prosecute three cases that would be tough to prove.

Or so it seemed.

WEDNESDAY, DECEMBER 11, 1985

Dennis Williams and Willie Rainge, who'd been moved to the county jail while the state decided whether to retry them, were playing Space Invaders in a dayroom when a fellow prisoner interrupted them.

"You might want to check this out," said the prisoner. He handed Williams a section of that morning's *Chicago Tribune* and pointed to a headline, "Man sentenced to death for 1978 double murder."

Williams's eyes dropped to the first paragraph of the story: "An East Chicago Heights man has been sentenced to death in connection with a double murder for which he was charged but escaped prosecution seven years ago."

Almost paralyzed, dreading to read further, Williams lowered the paper and audibly gasped.

"What is it, man?" Rainge asked.

Williams scanned the rest of the story, which confirmed his worst fear.

He read the second paragraph to Rainge: "After a two-hour death sentence hearing Monday in the [south suburban] Markham branch of the Cook County Circuit Court, Associate Judge Will Gierach ordered that Verneal Jimerson, thirty-three, be executed on April one, nineteen eighty-six."

"That ain't possible," said Rainge, grabbing the paper.

The story went on to say, "Jimerson was arrested with four others for the crime but was freed after one of them, Paula Gray, changed her testimony that implicated him. Last year, Gray again began cooperating with prosecutors, and Jimerson was rearrested in December, as a result of her statements."

"This is fucked up, man," said Rainge. "How come we didn't hear—"

Before Rainge could finish his question, Williams was running for a phone.

"Hi, Dennis," said Margaret Roberts, cheerfully accepting the collect call. "Great news, I'm coming to Chicago next month, and we'll finally be able to meet in person."

"Margaret, they're gonna murder Lurch."

"What? Who's going to murder Lurch?"

Williams told her about the story he'd just seen. "Maybe it's not true," he said, halfheartedly.

Roberts's mind flashed back to her interview three years earlier with Jimerson, in which he'd expressed fear that Paula might cave in. And she thought of the recent failure of the Grays to respond to her correspondence.

The *Tribune* story definitely was true, she knew, but she wanted to find out more before saying so to Williams.

"Let me call Rob," she said. "Get back to me in a little while."

■ ■ ■

"I was horrified when I saw the story," Rob Warden said. "Dumbfounded, too—I mean you'd think we would've heard."

Neither Verneal Jimerson nor his lawyer, whom Warden didn't know, had contacted *Chicago Lawyer*. And Warden had seen no news coverage of the case, perhaps because the trial had been in the far-south suburb of Markham, off the beaten path for the major media.

A few minutes before Roberts called, Warden had reached Isaiah "Skip" Gant, Dennis Williams's new lawyer, who'd also learned of Jimerson's death sentence from the *Tribune* story.

Gant, a private attorney appointed by the court to represent Williams at the taxpayers' expense, said he'd promptly request a copy of the trial transcript and share it with Warden.

"Did Gant say what this might mean for Dennis?" Roberts asked.

"I didn't have to ask him," Warden said. "It's obvious they'll retry him with Paula in their hip pocket again."

It was crucial, he said, to find out what prosecutors had offered Gray in return for her testimony—a question that the transcript should answer. But presumably any deal would include her testifying against Williams, and no doubt Willie Rainge as well.

Warden contemplated even worse possibilities: Prosecutors could cut a deal with Jimerson for a reduced sentence if he'd testify at the retrial. Gray's cooperation also gave prosecutors leverage to try to flip Rainge against Williams. Maybe even Kenny Adams finally would be broken after seven years in prison.

"Christ," said Roberts. "What can we do?"

"Get real drunk real fast," said Warden.

■ ■ ■

After reading the trial transcript, it was abundantly clear to Rob Warden how Verneal Jimerson had been convicted.

Paula Gray and Charles McCraney had sealed his fate, with more than a little help from the same prosecutors who'd won the 1978 convictions.

Under questioning by Assistant State's Attorney Scott Arthur, Gray had repeated the chilling story she'd told the grand jury seven years earlier. Jimerson's role in the crime, she testified, had been to rape Carol Schmal twice and to guard Larry Lionberg while the others raped her.

Gray continued that, after her grand jury appearance, she and her family had temporarily moved in with Dennis Williams's mother—a tacit explanation for her recantation.

But perhaps the most surprising thing about Gray's testimony was her categorical denial, under cross-examination by defense lawyer Earl Taylor, that prosecutors had offered her a deal.

"When do you expect to get out of jail, Paula?" Taylor asked.

"I don't know."

"Has anyone promised you anything for appearing here in court?"

"No."

"Were you told if you testified that you may get out of jail earlier?"

"No."

"No promises were made to you by Mr. Arthur at all?"

"No."

As questionable as her denial of a deal might have been, Gray's latest version of the crime was at least consistent with her grand jury testimony. McCraney's story, on the other hand, seemed to have improved with age.

In 1978, McCraney had been unable to place Jimerson at the scene of the crime. Now, under questioning by Assistant State's Attorney Clifford Johnson, he claimed Jimerson in fact had been there.

"On the evening of May ten, did you have occasion to see this individual, Verneal Jimerson?" Johnson asked.

"He was out front."

"And who was he with?"

"The rest of them. Rainge and all them."

McCraney still did not say that Jimerson had run into the abandoned townhouse with the others, but claimed he definitely saw Jimerson in the courtyard as late as midnight, and did not see him leave.

Moreover, McCraney had testified in 1978 that he had no clock. Now he claimed to have had two clocks, enabling him to say with more authority that he'd seen the group enter the townhouse after 3:00 A.M.

On cross-examination, Taylor inexplicably failed to bring out

McCraney's inconsistencies. He also failed to ask McCraney about the reward money from Clark Oil and relocation expenses from the state.

The remainder of the evidence, including the forensic testimony, was a virtual playback from 1978.

Arthur argued in closing that the crime was "so evil it has no precedent in this system of justice, a crime so horrendous that it is almost beyond belief."

On November 11, 1985, the jury deliberated four hours and eight minutes before finding Jimerson guilty.

At sentencing the following month, Judge Gierach asked Jimerson if he had anything to say.

"Never in my life have I hurt nobody," said Jimerson, "and I just want to say I am innocent."

Despite Jimerson's spotless record, Judge Gierach declared, "I find that there is no mitigation to preclude the imposition of the death penalty, and the defendant will be sentenced to die by lethal injection."

■ ■ ■

There were few things Scott Arthur and Clifford Johnson relished more than convicting Verneal Jimerson.

It had been unfinished business.

They had no doubt that Jimerson, like the others, was guilty.

And now that they'd proven it to a jury, they could focus on new responsibilities: Both had been appointed to executive jobs at the main criminal courts building in Chicago.

But Arthur, widely known as the more zealous of the two, had no intention of forsaking Markham, where he'd risen from a law clerk to supervisor of prosecutions.

He'd be back to lead the re-prosecutions of Dennis Williams and Willie Rainge. He owed it to the families of the murder victims, with whom he'd forged a deep personal bond. And he owed it to his Markham troops, a close-knit team of good guys who knew how to put bad guys on ice.

■ ■ ■

Not everyone appreciated Markham the way Scott Arthur did.

"A cross between Selma and Moscow," was Cook County Public Defender James Doherty's epithet for the place.

"It's like South Africa," said Kendall Hill, a black assistant public defender.

And the criticism wasn't restricted to the defense bar.

"Frankly, some of the prosecutors down here are like Nazis," said a black prosecutor assigned to Markham. "One of them told me anybody could convict a guilty man, but it took a real prosecutor to convict an innocent man."

A judge in the building reported that some Markham prosecutors tallied the weight of the black defendants convicted each week, referring to the exercise as "nigger by the pound."

"The elation over Verneal Jimerson's conviction was probably tempered because he brought down the week's average," said the judge, referring to the fact that Jimerson weighed in at only 142 pounds.

Part of the problem, the critics suggested to Rob Warden, was that Markham was an outpost, the regional court farthest from the central headquarters of the state's attorney's office and the circuit court. As such, it had developed its own clubbish culture.

In the inner circle were the judges, prosecutors, and south suburban cops, drawn overwhelmingly from white ethnic areas of Cook County.

On the fringe were private defense lawyers, for whom Markham was only an occasional whistle-stop, and public defenders, for whom it was a way station on the road to a better assignment.

Then there were the defendants, the ultimate outsiders.

They were disproportionately black, overwhelmingly poor, and often viewed as little more than cattle to be rendered or, as one prosecutor branded the four East Chicago Heights defendants, "scumbags."

■ ■ ■

Dennis Williams became enraged as he read the transcript of Verneal Jimerson's trial.

After an unsuccessful attempt to reach his lawyer, Williams called *Chicago Lawyer* and asked for Rob Warden.

Warden was out to lunch, but David Protess took the call.

Ever curious, Williams wanted to know who Protess was.

"I teach journalism at Northwestern, and I'm here working on a story about prosecutorial misconduct," said Protess, endearing himself immediately to Williams.

"You should look at our case," Williams said. "The prosecutors belong in prison for what they did."

Protess said he'd read about the case and might be interested in doing something later.

"Don't wait too long," Williams cautioned, "or me and one of my codefendants won't be around to see it."

Breaking the awkward silence that followed, Williams asked Protess just to relay a message that he hoped Warden would join Margaret Roberts when she visited him later that week.

"Uh, sure thing," Protess said.

When Warden returned, Protess was staring out the window.

"Writer's block?" Warden asked.

Protess told him about the call, explaining that he'd never talked to anyone in prison before, much less anyone who'd been sentenced to death.

"Plus, he's probably innocent," said Warden.

Protess began pacing.

Warden watched him, finally asking, "Wanna get involved?"

"I'm not sure, Rob," said Protess.

His ambivalence stemmed from a haunting childhood memory of the execution of Julius and Ethel Rosenberg in 1953. He'd been inspired by the worldwide effort to save them and devastated when it failed, orphaning two Jewish boys about his age.

The Rosenberg case had made him an ardent opponent of the death penalty and shaped his cynical view of the criminal justice system.

But it also had made him dread getting caught up in a capital case that could similarly end in tragedy.

"What if we prove that Dennis Williams is innocent, I mean truly innocent, and they kill him anyway? I don't know if I could handle that."

■ ■ ■

Wearing tan coveralls and smoking an unfiltered cigarette, Dennis Williams pressed his right hand against the Plexiglas barrier that separated him from his visitors.

Rob Warden and Margaret Roberts greeted him with prison handshakes, each in turn placing a hand on the cold surface opposite his.

Williams smiled broadly, but his eyes betrayed exhaustion and anxiety.

Speaking through a louvered metal plate, Williams said, in an uncharacteristic drawl, "I apologize for my appearance. I ain't slept hardly at all since Lurch got sentenced."

"You look fine, Dennis, just a little tired," Roberts told him.

Williams nodded appreciatively. "I'm tryin' to stay focused on my case, but it's hard to concentrate in here. Sometimes I think I'd rather be on Death Row, believe it or not."

He said the county jail, because of extreme crowding, was louder and more dangerous, in addition to which the food was worse. There were, however, a couple of advantages: He could spend time with Willie Rainge and occasionally see his mother and brother.

"Easier access to your lawyer, too," Warden chimed in.

Williams rolled his eyes. Although Skip Gant had come highly recommended by René Brown, who'd worked with Gant on the Pontiac prison riot case, Williams didn't like or trust him. "I can't never get him on the phone," said Williams, "and he's only been to see me once."

In their sole face-to-face meeting, they'd clashed over trial strategy. "Skip wants to base the defense on attacking Paula," Williams said, "and I want to subpoena Dennis Johnson and tear the state's whole case apart."

Fortunately, Williams said, the judge who'd appointed Gant also had approved using county funds to pay René Brown as the defense investigator. Williams hoped Brown would agree with his strategy.

"Maybe René can find out why Paula's cooperating with the prosecutors again," Roberts said. "I refuse to believe she doesn't have a deal."

"Oh, she's got one all right," Williams said. "She just lied about it, just like she lied on Lurch and us. She'll walk for sure as soon as she testifies against me and Tuna."

"And Scott Arthur will just sit on his goddamn hands again while she lies through her teeth," Warden said. "That makes him no better than she is."

Williams's eyes narrowed at the mention of Arthur. "I've struggled for a long time with my hatred for that man, trying to comprehend why he'd want to persecute us this way."

At first, Williams said, he'd thought Arthur was just a racist, pure and simple. But then Williams had begun reading books on psychology in the prison library. Erich Fromm and Alan Watts, among others, had convinced him that Arthur's motivation was more complex.

"He needs to dominate others," Williams said. "Scott Arthur is on a power trip. He's capable of rationalizing anything—even perjury, even murdering us—just to stay on top."

Arthur would never admit he'd made a mistake, Williams predicted. "The more he's challenged by evidence that we're innocent, the more determined he'll be to oppress us."

Becoming increasingly animated, Williams went on, "I knew bullies like him growing up, but this guy's got the power of the state behind him. He gets a thrill out of whuppin' us. To him, we're prey."

As Williams spoke, Roberts admired his growing intellectual insight but was chilled by the sense that he was confronting the prospect of his death, like a patient going through the psychological stages of a terminal illness. She wanted to reassure him, but didn't know quite what to say.

Warden, however, took Williams's commentary as a challenge, and more than ever wanted to take on Scott Arthur. If Arthur had suborned Gray's perjury and sponsored McCraney's shifting story, Warden said, perhaps the state had engaged in other contrivances.

Foremost in Warden's mind was the forensic evidence, and he proposed to find out whether the state's analysis of the blood evidence had been correct.

"There are three recent cases where the state fucked up big time on forensic evidence," he explained.

One was a murder case in which a state lab had mixed up the blood samples of two brothers. The others involved rapes in which state forensic scientists had grossly overstated the odds that semen had come from the defendants.

"In your case," Warden told Williams, "the state says the semen from Carol Schmal is consistent with your blood type and Kenny Adams's. We shouldn't assume that's true, because your lawyers never checked."

"How do we find out?" Williams asked.

"A simple saliva test. I'll arrange it and send you and Kenny the stuff you need to provide the samples. We can do it all by mail."

Williams quickly agreed.

Warden also told Williams that he'd struck upon another idea to attack the state's case with forensics: laboratory tests on Bic-type lighters.

While it seemed unlikely that Paula Gray could have held a lighter burning almost continuously for half an hour while four men committed seven rapes, her claim hadn't been scientifically tested. Warden was looking for an expert to do that.

"Who's gonna pay for all this?" Williams asked.

"It won't cost that much," Warden replied. "*Chicago Lawyer* will cover it."

"If I'm ever in a position to pay you back, I will," Williams promised.

The three spent their remaining time together talking of Warden's recent marriage, Roberts's life in Washington, and Williams's latest passion, oil painting.

"The reason I like oils is that they don't dry right away, like watercolors do," he said. "You can shape and mold your images."

He said he was taking instruction from a prisoner named Jesse Owens, who was awaiting trial for assault and battery.

"Jesse Owens?" Roberts chuckled. "Is he teaching you how to sprint and jump, too?"

"Yeah," Williams shot back with a raspy laugh, "right over the wall."

■ ■ ■

Kenny Adams called collect from the Menard Correctional Center in response to a letter from Rob Warden and agreed at once to the saliva test.

It was a brief conversation because Adams was a "neutron" in a prison almost totally controlled by gangs and, consequently, had severely limited access to a phone.

But they talked long enough for Adams to say that before Verneal Jimerson's trial he'd been visited by investigators from the state's attorney's office, who'd suggested in no uncertain terms that he could get out if he'd testify.

He'd flatly turned them down, but expected they'd be back now that a new trial was looming for Dennis Williams and Willie Rainge.

"They just don't get it," he sighed.

■ ■ ■

Checking around for an expert to test disposable cigarette lighters, Rob Warden was referred to L. J. Broutman & Associates, a lab affiliated with the Illinois Institute of Technology.

Warden arranged for Dr. Paul K. So, a senior scientist at Broutman, to conduct videotaped tests on five disposable lighters: two Bics, two Scriptos, and a Cricket.

The Bics extinguished in less than eight minutes when their metal tops detached upon reaching 277 degrees.

The Scriptos melted and went out in less than ten minutes at 321 degrees.

Only the Cricket burned for half an hour, but it reached a temperature of 294 degrees in six minutes and its nozzle valve disintegrated.

■ ■ ■

Dr. Edward T. Blake, a Berkeley-educated serologist who headed Forensic Science Associates in Richmond, California, agreed to test saliva samples from Dennis Williams and Kenny Adams.

Rob Warden mailed each prisoner a zip-lock plastic bag and a cotton ball, with instructions to saturate the cotton with saliva, let it dry, seal it in the bag, and send it to Blake.

Blake was pioneering the application of DNA technology to criminal cases, but that science was still in its infancy in 1986, so he used conventional tests known as "absorption inhibition" and "absorption elution."

He found that both Williams and Adams indeed had type A

blood. Contrary to the state's forensic testimony at the 1978 trial, however, Williams was a nonsecretor, which meant he couldn't have been the source of the A blood antigens in the semen recovered from Carol Schmal.

Adams was a secretor, but an unusually weak one, and Blake thought it doubtful that Adams alone could have accounted for the A antigens in the semen.

Bottom line: It was unlikely that any of the four men had raped Carol Schmal.

To be certain, however, Blake told Warden he would have to do more tests. He wanted a fresh blood sample from Adams to be sure his secretions were as weak as they appeared. He wanted the vaginal swab from Schmal to recheck the level of A antigens. And he wanted to confirm that Willie Rainge, Verneal Jimerson, and Larry Lionberg all had type O blood, as the state had found.

"That'll take a court order and cooperation from lawyers for all the defendants," Warden said.

"If I were them, I'd go for it," Blake said. "I think there's a decent chance the tests will prove they're all innocent."

7

"Let's Have a Little Conspiracy"

▪ The retrial of Dennis Williams and Willie Rainge, scheduled to begin in the summer of 1986, was abruptly postponed when Dr. Edward Blake dropped his forensic bombshell at a pretrial hearing.

With court approval, Blake had tested fresh blood and saliva samples from Williams, confirming that he couldn't have been the source of the semen on the vaginal swab from Carol Schmal.

"We're going to retest *all* the goddamn scientific evidence," an angry Scott Arthur told Rob Warden after the hearing.

"Fine," said Warden with a shrug.

A few weeks later, a state scientist reexamined the hair evidence in the case. His conclusion: The hairs recovered from Williams's Toyota didn't match the hair of Carol Schmal or Larry Lionberg.

Since this finding contradicted the state's contention in 1978, when three of the hairs were said to match, Arthur was now forced to abandon the hair evidence.

The blood evidence, meanwhile, was tested by London's Scotland Yard at Arthur's request. More bad news: Williams indeed was a nonsecretor. Blake had been right.

Scotland Yard also confirmed that Kenny Adams was an A secretor, but wasn't able to rule him in or out as a possible source of the semen. Unlike in 1978, this time no A antigens were found on the vaginal swab: Either the state's test had been inaccurate or the antigens had deteriorated over the years.

Bottom line: With both Scotland Yard and Blake now questioning the original blood evidence, Scott Arthur had no choice but to drop it, too.

He could only hope the defense lawyers would do the same.

■ ■ ■

Isaiah "Skip" Gant had just about had it with Dennis Williams.

In ten years of practicing law, Gant had encountered his share of difficult clients, including the Pontiac prison rioters.

But Williams was in a class by himself.

After a series of disagreements over trial strategy, Williams had rudely written to Frank Meekins, the Markham trial judge assigned to the case, calling Gant incompetent.

Meekins had put the impudent client in his place, saying Gant was "one of the absolute very finest attorneys in the state of Illinois."

That, however, hadn't deterred Williams, who threatened to fire Gant and act as his own lawyer.

Now Williams was demanding that Gant arrange for independent forensic testing, failing to understand that the state no longer had any scientific evidence and it was better simply to leave the matter alone.

Besides, Gant thought Judge Meekins would never approve the expense of additional testing. Gant didn't expect any breaks from this judge, who'd formerly been the village prosecutor of Glenwood, the suburb where Carol Schmal had been raised.

Victory, in Gant's view, would depend on selecting a fair jury, exposing Paula Gray as the liar she surely was, and attacking Charles McCraney's inconsistencies. Hell, McCraney hadn't seen any white people at the abandoned townhouse, and he'd placed the defendants there before the victims had even been abducted.

Gant believed he had enough evidence to create reasonable doubt, his only goal.

Williams wanted outright exoneration, but that wasn't a defense lawyer's job.

Besides, Gant had other things on his mind.

He was hobbled with a broken leg that had required surgery.

And the IRS was breathing down his neck because he'd neglected to file tax returns for the last five years.

He'd just as soon let Williams represent himself.

But he needed the money.

■ ■ ■

Dennis Williams had thought Archie Weston was bad until he got Skip Gant.

Gant wouldn't listen to reason, when he'd listen at all.

Williams was confident that Dr. Blake could exonerate him. After all, Blake had already exposed the phony blood evidence. But Gant wasn't pursuing the additional tests Blake had proposed. If that cost money, Gant should demand it from the court. This was a capital case!

Gant also seemed to have reduced René Brown to a bit player in the trial preparations.

Brown hadn't interviewed Dennis Johnson since 1982 or pursued the other three men Johnson had claimed were involved in the crime.

Nor had Brown contacted two witnesses who could testify that Williams and Verneal Jimerson hadn't bolted from the crowd on the day the bodies were discovered. Williams had given Gant their names, but no one had followed up.

Then there was David Jackson, the jailhouse snitch. Brown

hadn't contacted him, either. Since Jackson no longer faced any criminal charges, maybe he wouldn't be willing to lie again about hearing Williams and Willie Rainge talking about the crime.

When Williams demanded to know why Brown wasn't going after important witnesses, Gant said Brown had developed a severe drinking problem that made him unreliable.

Williams had heard from family members that Brown had a fondness for beer and bourbon, but none of them thought the drinking affected his work.

"Look, we don't need René," said Gant. "The case hinges on Gray and McCraney."

"What about Dennis Johnson?" Williams asked.

"So," Gant responded contemptuously, "you wanna pin the crime on *other* brothers?"

"Yeah, if they did it."

At an impasse with Gant, Williams railed about the problem to Rainge, who was equally unhappy with his lawyer, Maurice Scott.

Scott had gotten into the case by approaching Rainge's family in the courthouse hallway and offering his services. Because the family was indigent, Judge Meekins approved paying Scott with public funds.

Rainge became disillusioned with his lawyer almost immediately. Scott left it to Rainge to contact Patricia Hatten, his principal alibi for the night of the crime. When Hatten expressed reluctance to testify, Scott dropped the matter, refusing to subpoena her.

Following Williams's lead, Rainge wrote to Judge Meekins complaining about Scott. The judge called Rainge's letter "totally nonsensical," adding, "I take it as a personal insult when you make comments about a lawyer of Mr. Maurice Scott's caliber."

As jury selection approached, Williams thought the situation was desperate. He wanted to get rid of Gant at any cost, but didn't want to represent himself.

In discussing what to do, Williams advanced a radical proposal:

When Gant came to see him before the next court hearing, he would slug him—just once, upside the head. Williams would do this in front of sheriff's deputies, so Gant could neither exaggerate nor deny what happened.

"No, man, you can't do that," Rainge counseled. "It'll just make things worse for us."

"It can't get any worse," Williams responded, but he promised to keep his hands off his lawyer.

■ ■ ■

Upon returning to his cell, Dennis Williams had an eerie feeling that something terrible had happened.

The next morning, he asked a guard for special permission to call home, where he got the news: His mother had passed away after suffering a stroke.

He'd hoped she would live to see him a free man, but now he wouldn't even be allowed to attend her funeral.

In her final visit two weeks earlier, she'd reassured him that no matter what the outcome of the trial, the truth someday would prevail. As she'd put it, "What doesn't come out in the wash will come out in the rinse."

FEBRUARY 1987

In the Markham courtroom of Judge Frank Meekins, prosecutors and defense lawyers jockeyed for three days over the composition of the jury.

Scott Arthur used most of the prosecution's peremptory challenges to excuse eleven blacks.

The defense vociferously objected that Arthur had violated a 1986 U.S. Supreme Court decision barring racial discrimination in jury selection, but Meekins held otherwise.

On February 4, a jury of nine whites and three blacks was impaneled to hear the case.

In opening statements that afternoon, Arthur dwelt on the horrific nature of the crime, while the defense attacked the credibility of the police and eyewitnesses.

"Dennis Williams took Carol Schmal to an abandoned, rat-infested townhouse where he ordered her to take her clothes off and proceeded to engage in a vicious act of lustful rape," said Arthur, pacing in front of the jury box.

Wearing slacks and a sports jacket, the prosecutor walked in a pattern, looking down at the floor at times, hands jammed into his pockets, seeming to calculate where he was going to take his next step, make his next point.

"She was raped twice by Dennis Williams, raped twice by Willie Rainge, raped twice by Verneal Jimerson, raped once by Kenny Adams," he said, his piercing blue eyes fixed on the jury. "During this period of time, Dennis and his little band would hold Carol's fiancé, Larry, at bay downstairs in the same townhouse."

Pointing at the defendants, Arthur asserted that the state would show that Williams had fired four of the five shots that ended the couple's lives, and Rainge had fired the fifth.

Isaiah Gant, bearded and wearing a gray sharkskin suit with a white carnation on the lapel, countered that there was "no credible evidence" linking Dennis Williams to the crime.

Paula Gray's incriminating story, he said, "came about as a result of some very, very suspicious conduct on the part of the police." She was a convicted perjurer, he pointed out, claiming that she'd now flip-flopped because she wanted to get out of prison.

Maurice Scott, dressed in a brown suit and crisp white shirt, was brief, substantively adding only that the state's other principal witness, Charles McCraney, couldn't seem to get his story straight and had been imprecise in his description of Willie Rainge.

While both defense lawyers promised to expose weaknesses in

the state's case, they didn't offer to explain where their clients had been on the night of the crime.

■ ■ ■

Speaking in a soft voice, Paula Gray responded to Scott Arthur's questions with precise, detailed answers. She seemed to be reliving the crime, describing the dimensions of the room where Carol Schmal had died and the order in which the defendants had raped her. The victims had been shaking throughout the ordeal, she testified.

Under cross-examination by Skip Gant, however, she became extremely evasive. When asked if she'd claimed at the 1978 preliminary hearing that the police made her lie, she answered, "I don't remember." She gave the same answer when asked if she recalled testifying that the police had threatened to "whip my motherfucking ass."

Gray's memory loss extended even to very recent events. Had she met with Scott Arthur that morning? "I don't remember." How had she gotten from the jail to the courthouse? "I don't remember." Did she recall saying just minutes earlier on direct examination that she'd been before the grand jury in 1978? "I don't know."

She didn't equivocate, however, when Maurice Scott asked her, "You're testifying here in the hope of receiving leniency on your sentence, isn't that correct?"

"No, sir," she said.

Gray was excused without being confronted with a crucial fact that Arthur had acknowledged at a pretrial hearing: He'd agreed to drop the murder charges against her in exchange for her testimony.

Nor did the defense elicit her history of mental illness, including the acute schizophrenic reaction she'd suffered after her grand jury testimony.

Following Gray, the prosecution called Charles McCraney.

Assistant State's Attorney Deborah Dooling, second chairing Arthur, skillfully turned a potential embarrassment—the money McCraney had received from the state—to her tactical advantage. Acknowledging that the amount had risen to $3,600, she asked why he'd been paid.

"Because," McCraney replied, "I'd been approached by three men—"

Gant strenuously objected, hoping to prevent McCraney from claiming he'd been threatened. After a sidebar, the judge allowed McCraney to testify that he'd been paid relocation expenses, but not to say why.

Dooling managed to make her point in another way, asking McCraney why he'd been reluctant to come forward in the first place.

"The safety of my family," McCraney blurted out before Gant could object.

As the direct continued, Gant repeatedly objected and demanded sidebars, to the obvious annoyance of the judge.

Each time Gant rose to object, Meekins bounced the eraser of his pencil on the bench. He was skillful at pencil gymnastics, sometimes flipping it in a kind of triple gainer, other times bouncing it off his desk and back into his hand. At one point, after Gant demanded three sidebars in rapid succession, Meekins bounced the pencil so hard that it was launched into the center of the courtroom.

Gant's cross-examination plowed little new ground except on the issue of McCraney's clock ownership. McCraney, who'd testified in 1978 that he had no clock and in 1985 that he had two clocks, now claimed to have had one clock. When Gant zeroed in on the inconsistency, McCraney responded, "I possibly could have made a mistake."

But McCraney held firm on the time that he had seen the defendants run into the abandoned townhouse: "in the neighborhood of 3:15."

The other state witnesses, including police officers and relatives of the victims, repeated the testimony they'd given at the previous trials. The clean-cut David Capelli, still a south suburban sheriff's investigator, told how officers' "suspicions" had led to the arrests of Williams and Jimerson. And Carol Schmal's sister Lynn closed the state's case with tearful memories of the last time she'd seen Carol alive.

■ ■ ■

After a week of prosecution testimony, the defense case was remarkably brief, lasting little more than a day and including only five witnesses.

The first was Laurie Martino, personnel manager for A&R Security Services, who testified that Charles McCraney had worked there briefly in 1978 but had been terminated for "excessive absenteeism."

Next was Dr. Paul K. So, who described his experiments with disposable lighters.

On cross-examination, Arthur made the point that the Cricket was still burning when the test was stopped after thirty minutes. The defense could have elicited that the Cricket had reached 294 degrees in only six minutes, but Dr. So was excused without a redirect examination.

Dennis Williams and Willie Rainge just shook their heads.

During a break in the proceedings, they voiced their disgust to Skip Gant and Maurice Scott.

Both defendants wanted to take the stand, as they had in 1978, but the lawyers argued against it. "You'd make bad witnesses," said Skip Gant. "Your hostility would show through and put off the jurors." Maurice Scott argued that they'd already established reasonable doubt, and it was best not to risk testifying.

"How about me testifying?" implored Williams's brother James, who'd joined the conversation. "I could tell 'em about Dennis Johnson. He was at my house, talkin' about the crime."

"Forget it," Gant shot back. "The jury would think you're biased."

"But, I—" James Williams stammered.

"Shut up," Gant interrupted. "This is *my* case."

When court resumed a few minutes later, Gant called John Adams, a civil engineer with the Illinois State Water Survey, who testified that the flow of Deer Creek was far too slow to have washed away the murder weapon.

Adams was followed by Ronald Kurth, an Indiana police officer who'd led an underwater search of Deer Creek for the gun. Under questioning by Gant, Kurth said that eleven divers had systematically searched the creek, but the weapon hadn't been found.

On cross-examination by Arthur, however, Kurth testified that the Cook County Sheriff's Police had trolled the murky creek with a brick-sized magnet, which had broken off its line and sunk. Not only couldn't the divers find the gun. They couldn't find the magnet.

The testimony, which bolstered the possibility that Paula Gray had told the truth about what happened to the gun, caught Gant and Scott by surprise. They hadn't interviewed Kurth before putting him on the stand.

The only other defense witness was an official court reporter, who read prior inconsistent statements by Gray and McCraney into the record.

Without calling a single alibi witness, the defense rested.

In his closing argument, Gant said, "What this case boils down to is the testimony of Paula Gray and Charles McCraney." Gray was "a product of coercion," he said, and McCraney had modified his testimony on key points.

To dramatize the absence of forensic evidence, Gant got down on his hands and knees to illustrate the position that a rapist would have assumed, inevitably leaving palm- and fingerprints on the bedroom floor.

"Did you ever hear one shred of evidence to indicate that they took fingerprints from the scene?" he asked. "Did you ever hear one shred of testimony that they examined the vaginal cavity of this woman for seminal fluid and then matched it with any of these men's blood type?"

Maurice Scott's closing argument was built on a hunch: the unlikelihood that Larry Lionberg would have stood by passively while his fiancée was raped and murdered.

He pointed out that, according to Gray, Lionberg had been alone downstairs with Rainge, a much smaller man who was unarmed. "Do you think Lionberg would just stand there and shake?" he asked. "There were no doors. You could just run right out."

In rebuttal, Arthur mocked the defense. "Maybe the police made up all this evidence," he said. "Maybe the police decided: 'Let's have a little conspiracy. Let's get Dennis Williams. Let's get Willie Rainge, Kenny Adams, and Verneal Jimerson.'

"That's too far-fetched. If you find the defendants innocent, don't do it because Mr. Gant can get down on his knees here and tell you how his palms are when they're on the floor. Do it because you believe the police framed these men—because that's what you would have to believe now."

After being instructed by Judge Meekins, the jury began its deliberations.

It was Friday the thirteenth of February—Dennis Williams's thirtieth birthday.

■ ■ ■

Confident of victory, Skip Gant predicted there'd be a verdict by 10:00 P.M. "That way it will be on the TV news," he told Rob Warden. "Dennis and Willie will be found innocent."

Members of the defendants' families, putting their faith in a higher authority, solemnly joined hands and bowed their heads outside the courtroom.

"Please, dear Lord, Willie and Dennis need you," prayed Willie

Rainge's grandmother, Lilly Collins. "Please bless them and the jury, and the judge, and the lawyers. Give them all the courage and the strength to do what's right."

At 9:34 P.M., a buzzer in Judge Meekins's chambers rang, notifying him that the jury had reached a verdict after deliberating one hour and forty-four minutes.

As the jury filed into the courtroom, Meekins popped a cough drop into his mouth and asked, "Mr. Foreman, has the jury arrived at its verdict?"

"We have, your honor."

The verdicts were read by a court clerk: Dennis Williams, guilty on all counts. Willie Rainge, guilty on all counts.

A slight smile crossed Scott Arthur's face.

Williams locked eyes with him, glaring.

Then the defendants were handcuffed and led from the slowly emptying courtroom.

Willie Rainge's grandmother walked alone down the sterile corridor of the Markham courthouse.

"Oh, Lord, I haven't lost faith," she declared. "I still believe. Oh, Lord, I still believe."

■ ■ ■

After brief hearings the following month, Judge Frank Meekins prescribed the same punishments his predecessor had imposed—life without parole for Willie Rainge, death for Dennis Williams.

The only surprise came when, at Williams's sentencing hearing, Dennis Johnson's name surfaced in court for the first time.

Martin Carlson, one of Williams's former appellate lawyers, testified that he'd interviewed Johnson in 1980 at the home of James Williams.

Under questioning by Skip Gant, Carlson said, "In general,

Johnson told me that he knew who committed the murders [and] who abducted the two people from the gas station." Carlson also indicated that René Brown had information about the man who had sold Johnson the murder weapon a few days after the crime.

However, Carlson's testimony was limited because he hadn't been present when Johnson admitted his own role in the crime to René Brown, James Williams, and, later, Margaret Roberts—all of whom Gant refused to call as witnesses.

In a devastating cross-examination, Scott Arthur asked, "Who shot Larry Lionberg and Carol Schmal, Mr. Carlson?"

"I have no idea," said Carlson.

"Who did René Brown say Dennis Johnson bought the gun from, supposedly?"

"Mr. Brown did not give me that information."

"Do you know if [*Chicago Lawyer*] was aware that René Brown had the name of the person who supposedly shot Carol Schmal?"

"I do not."

"Do you know if Mr. Gant has the name of the person who supposedly shot Carol Schmal?"

"I do not."

"Did you ever tell Mr. Gant that René Brown has the name of the guy that really did this?"

"I don't believe we discussed that."

"Mr. Carlson, after you spoke to Dennis Johnson, did you call the police or the state's attorney's office?"

"No, I did not."

Carlson was excused.

The only other witnesses called by Gant were two members of the Illinois Coalition Against the Death Penalty.

In an impassioned closing argument, Arthur called the defense testimony "laughable, shameful, and absolutely unbelievable."

Meekins apparently agreed. The evidence, he said, "led to one, and only one, inescapable conclusion, and I accordingly find that there are no mitigating factors sufficient to preclude the imposition of a death sentence upon the defendant."

■ ■ ■

Margaret Roberts took the news as a personal failure.

"Look at what we've accomplished after five years," she told Rob Warden. "Now we've got two innocent men on Death Row."

She still believed that the media could be a force for justice and, in fact, was about to take a job where she thought that would be possible, as a producer for *America's Most Wanted.*

■ ■ ■

The trustees of East Chicago Heights, dismayed that the village's image had been tarnished by the continuing coverage of the case and by reports of skyrocketing crime and unemployment, took decisive action on March 1, 1987.

They changed the name of the suburb to Ford Heights.

■ ■ ■

Seven weeks after sentencing Dennis Williams to death, Judge Meekins dismissed the murder charges against Paula Gray at the request of the prosecution.

By agreement, he gave her two years' probation for perjuring herself in 1978, when she'd testified she knew nothing about the murders of Larry Lionberg and Carol Schmal.

On April 23, Paula Gray packed her belongings and went home to her family in Ford Heights.

8

To the Windmill

■ "I want you to save a man's life," Professor Albert Alschuler told his former University of Chicago law student, Mark Ter Molen, in the spring of 1991.

The man Alschuler wanted saved was Verneal Jimerson, whose conviction had been affirmed by a six-to-one vote of the Illinois Supreme Court. (Seymour Simon had retired from the court, and Justice William G. Clark had been the lone dissenter, commenting that the prosecution had "relied almost entirely on the testimony of Paula Gray, a witness whose credibility was—to put it mildly—subject to question.")

Ter Molen, whose name means "to the windmill" in Dutch, was a twenty-nine-year-old associate at Chicago's second largest law firm, Mayer, Brown & Platt.

"I'm looking for a feel-good project," said Ter Molen, who regarded Alschuler as a mentor.

Ter Molen had just won a major *pro bono* case—asylum for a Honduran political refugee—and was anxious for another.

While Ter Molen favored the death penalty in certain circumstances, he agreed with Alschuler that Jimerson seemed an inappropriate candidate. Even if he'd participated in the crime, he hadn't been a triggerman and had no criminal history.

There was a good chance the firm would give him permission to take the case, said Ter Molen. Major Chicago law firms were increasingly handling capital appeals as the number of Death Row prisoners swelled, and Mayer, Brown & Platt wanted to share the load.

After studying the case file and speaking with a senior partner, Ter Molen called Alschuler back.

"We'll do it," he said.

■ ■ ■

Shortly after Mark Ter Molen took the Jimerson case, the convictions of Dennis Williams and Willie Rainge were unanimously affirmed: Williams's by the Illinois Supreme Court, Rainge's by the Illinois Appellate Court. Both courts rejected claims similar to those raised by Verneal Jimerson.

The Williams opinion was written by Justice Charles E. Freeman, the first African-American member of the court, who'd been elected to Justice Simon's former seat.

Freeman rejected Williams's claims that the evidence had been insufficient to prove guilt beyond a reasonable doubt, that African-Americans had been improperly excluded from the jury, and that Isaiah Gant had rendered ineffective assistance of counsel.

Concerning Gant's failure to investigate the alternative suspects, Freeman wrote: "Any continued investigation to procure Dennis Johnson, an alleged witness to the crimes, would certainly prove fruitless."

The opinion didn't mention Gant's legal problems, even though he'd pleaded guilty in 1989 to five counts of willfully failing to file federal income tax returns.

Gant's problems were well known to the court because the issue had been raised in Williams's brief, and the court itself had recently upheld the suspension of his law license.

Williams's execution was set for January 28, 1992, a date that would be delayed by further appeals.

■ ■ ■

Rob Warden watched the developments from the sidelines, frustrated over events he was powerless to affect.

In 1989, he'd sold the deficit-ridden *Chicago Lawyer* to the Law Bulletin Publishing Company, which shunned muckraking.

Warden's final cover story had blasted the Cook County State's Attorney's Office for burying evidence that two African-Americans had been wrongly convicted of a 1983 murder.

Elton Houston and Robert Brown had served five years in prison for killing a filling station attendant when Thomas Peters, their attorney, discovered secret police notes—"street files"—revealing that another man had confessed to the crime.

As Warden packed up his office, he felt that he'd spent a decade beating his head against a wall of official malfeasance. While *Chicago Lawyer* had brought many injustices to public attention, Warden was disgusted that the same problems kept resurfacing.

"These stories are like pissing in the ocean," he told David Protess. "You make a little splash, but nothing really changes and nobody cares."

Still hoping to challenge the status quo—this time as an insider—Warden became the issues director for Jack O'Malley's 1990 campaign for Cook County State's Attorney.

Promising to make the office "the fairest prosecutor's office in the country," O'Malley waged an aggressive campaign against the incumbent, an elderly Democratic machine boss.

After O'Malley won the November election, Warden did not immediately join the new administration. At that time, his presence in an office that he'd so often attacked might have strengthened internal resistance to reform.

Unemployed, biding his time, Warden succumbed to a plea from David Protess to join him in an investigation of a possible miscarriage of justice, the conviction of a working-class suburban man named David Dowaliby.

Dowaliby had been sentenced in 1990 to forty-five years in prison for the murder of his seven-year-old daughter, Jaclyn, who'd vanished from her bed in the middle of the night and had been found strangled four days later.

Warden and Protess developed new evidence, including the recantation of the state's star witness, that helped exonerate Dowaliby. Protess's students assisted in the investigation, and Jenner & Block—the firm that was representing Girvies Davis—handled Dowaliby's case *pro bono*.

When Warden and Protess began writing a book about the case, they were repeatedly interrupted by collect calls from prisoners who'd seen media coverage of Dowaliby's release from prison.

The most frequent caller was Dennis Williams, imploring them not to forget his case.

Warden listened sympathetically, but he and Protess had a book to finish.

Finally, they stopped answering the phone.

■ ■ ■

Gearing up for the fight to save Verneal Jimerson, Mark Ter Molen prevailed on two other young Mayer, Brown & Platt associates, Jonathan Olcott and Fredrick Levin, to work on the case.

The trio's work would be augmented by investigative and legal support from the Illinois Capital Resource Center, a state agency that provided assistance to indigent defendants on Death Row.

The Jimerson team was up against it because the next step in the arduous appellate process would be to file a petition for a new trial in perhaps the unfriendliest of forums: the court that had convicted him.

Ter Molen's strategy was to put a massive effort into the petition, not only expecting to lose before Judge Will Gierach, but in fact hoping to lose without even a hearing. Gierach surely wouldn't reverse himself in a case in which he'd imposed a death sentence that already had been affirmed by the Illinois Supreme Court. But if the team put together a persuasive petition that Gierach didn't take seriously enough to grant a hearing, the supreme court might consider him unfair and take a hard look at the case.

In preparing the petition, the team focused first on the woeful performance of Earl Taylor, Jimerson's trial lawyer.

The Jimerson family, believing a private lawyer was preferable to a public defender, had hired Taylor. When family funds were exhausted, Judge Gierach had appointed him to continue at county expense.

Taylor made no excuses when he was contacted by Raymond Prusak, an attorney working under the auspices of the Capital Resource Center. Driven by a guilty conscience, Taylor freely acknowledged his ineffectiveness in a sworn statement.

"This case was the first and only capital case that I have tried as an attorney [and] I have never attended any seminars on defending clients in capital cases," Taylor said.

"I did not effectively cross-examine the state's chief witness, Paula Gray," he continued. "During the cross-examination I became flustered by her responses [and] sat down too early, before fully completing the cross-examination."

Taylor further acknowledged that he hadn't even read much of the earlier testimony of Gray and Charles McCraney.

Finally, he said, "I thought that the trial judge would not impose the death penalty on my client and [I] went through the motions at the sentencing hearing, thinking it was a 'lay down' and that the trial judge would sentence my client to life imprisonment."

Ter Molen's team gathered affidavits from twenty of Jimerson's acquaintances and relatives who would have testified at the sentencing hearing as to his good character, but who weren't contacted by Taylor.

The Reverend Charles Nelson, the only witness Taylor did call at the hearing, provided an affidavit saying his testimony could have been far stronger. However, Taylor had failed to interview Nelson before he took the stand.

The team also discovered that Taylor's law license had once been suspended due to "a pattern of consistent neglect" in his work on behalf of clients. In one criminal case, he'd failed to appear at the trial and, after the client won the case himself, Taylor refused to return the fee he'd been paid.

■ ■ ■

While Earl Taylor's shortcomings as an advocate saddened Mark Ter Molen, Scott Arthur's performance as a prosecutor infuriated him.

It was bad enough that Arthur would cut a deal with Paula Gray under any circumstances. But worse, Ter Molen discovered, Arthur had allowed Gray to lie about it under oath.

Ter Molen's team had made this discovery in a careful review of court records from the retrial of Dennis Williams and Willie Rainge.

In response to a written request from Williams and Rainge's defense lawyers, Arthur had acknowledged that the murder charges against Gray would be dropped in exchange for her testimony.

Under the law, Arthur also should have disclosed the deal to Earl Taylor, but had failed to do so. And when Gray denied under oath that she'd been promised anything, Arthur had a professional obligation to correct her perjury.

Arthur couldn't dodge responsibility for the improprieties, Ter Molen knew, because the proof was in black and white: Arthur's signature was on the document acknowledging the deal, and it *pre-dated* the Jimerson trial.

Ter Molen's petition for a new trial would include an incontrovertible claim of prosecutorial misconduct.

■ ■ ■

Mark Ter Molen had never been inside a prison when he went to the Pontiac Correctional Center, where the state had established a second Death Row to accommodate the overflow from Menard.

A guard ushered the sandy-haired, blue-eyed lawyer into the visiting area, a vast room resembling a high school cafeteria, with Formica tables and attached plastic chairs.

Ter Molen craned his neck in search of his client among the mob of manacled prisoners and guests. He had virtually no idea what Verneal Jimerson looked like, having seen only his mug shot. He hoped Jimerson wasn't the immense, tattooed inmate who first caught his eye, and was relieved when the man scowled and looked away.

Then, in the midst of the hubbub, Ter Molen spotted a small, bespectacled prisoner reading a book. Ter Molen drew near and introduced himself to the quiet man known as Lurch.

He'd picked up the nickname, Jimerson explained, because he resembled, in demeanor if not in size, the popular character from *The Addams Family*.

Jimerson was born in rural Arkansas, where his parents were sharecroppers, before they moved to East Chicago Heights in 1965 with their twelve children.

Growing up, he sang in the choir of the Trinity Church of God in Christ. His mother's dream was that he would become a preacher, like the Reverend Nelson.

Jimerson did odd jobs around the church and worked at a car wash, where he was employed full-time upon graduating from Bloom High School.

Since entering prison, he'd suffered the loss of his parents: his father in 1986, his mother in 1990. Missing their funerals had made the pain all the worse.

After the Illinois Supreme Court denied his appeal, he'd told his wife to move on with her life. She and their three daughters had moved to Pittsburgh, where her family lived, making visits financially impossible.

But Jimerson had accepted his fate. "God put me in prison for a reason," he told Ter Molen, "and that is to teach the other guys about His love."

When the conversation turned to the facts of the case, Jimerson recounted that he'd been in East Chicago Heights on May 10, 1978, but that Dennis Williams had driven him home to Chicago several hours before the crime occurred.

Just as they arrived, they heard on the radio that a new Herbie Hancock record would be played after a commercial break. Jimerson said good night and hurried inside to listen, leaving his sunglasses in the car.

Jimerson next saw Williams two days later, in the crowd that had gathered after the bodies were found. "If I hadn't gone to Dennis's car to get my shades back, all this wouldn't have happened," he said.

Jimerson noted that he was only casually acquainted with the other men convicted of the crime because he'd been four years ahead of them in school. He'd played softball with Dennis Williams and attended church with Kenny Adams and Willie Rainge.

The first time the four of them were ever together, he believed, was at a bond hearing after they were arrested. And he'd never even laid eyes on Paula Gray until the preliminary hearing, when she said the police had made her lie.

After two hours, it became apparent to Ter Molen that his client seemed utterly baffled by what had happened to him.

Ter Molen explained that a long and complicated process lay ahead, and that he would keep him informed at every step.

"Do whatever has to be done," Jimerson said softly in parting. "I have faith."

■ ■ ■

Dennis Williams shared Verneal Jimerson's faith in God, but not in lawyers.

Williams was waiting for the Capital Resource Center to assign counsel to his case. But he, unlike Jimerson, wouldn't be getting *pro bono* help. He'd only have lawyers paid by the taxpayers, as Skip Gant had been. "That makes them agents of the state," Williams wrote Rob Warden.

From initial conversations, it seemed to Williams that the agency's staff didn't believe he was innocent and just hoped to set aside his death sentence on a technicality.

"They want to make me out to be guilty but crazy, rather than exposing a scandal of this magnitude," said the letter. "I may be burning with justifiable rage, but I'm certainly not insane."

Williams believed he could be exonerated by newly developed DNA technology. The vaginal swab from Carol Schmal had been preserved, and Williams wanted to get a court order allowing Dr. Edward Blake to test it.

But his new lawyers, he predicted, "will not do anything to bring about my rightfully deserved freedom."

In his view, whoever the agency found to represent him would take the case just for the money. "I am about to be auctioned off by the legal system," he wrote, "but lethal injection will not intimidate me into going along with a strategy that makes me appear guilty just to save my life."

Hoping that Jenner & Block might step in, as it had for Girvies Davis and David Dowaliby, Williams asked Warden for the name of someone to contact at the firm.

As far as the Capital Resource Center was concerned, he declared: "I disavow anything they plan to do, will not cooperate, nor will I accept any visits from any attorney assigned by their office. That's absolutely final."

The letter closed, "In liberty's name, Dennis."

■ ■ ■

Meeting Verneal Jimerson raised the stakes for Mark Ter Molen, who became consumed with the fight to get his gentle client off Death Row.

Fretting over the possibility of failure, having never handled a criminal case, Ter Molen turned to a friend with experience in criminal law, Jeanne Bishop.

Bishop's experience was both professional and painfully personal: In 1990, her sister and brother-in-law, Nancy and Richard Langert, had been murdered in their home in the upscale Chicago suburb of Winnetka.

Nancy, three months pregnant, had been shot in the abdomen. After watching her husband shot execution-style in the head, too weak to call for help, she drew—in her own blood—a heart and the letter *u*, for "love you." Then she died.

Grieving over their deaths, Bishop had been further traumatized by FBI and police leaks suggesting that she was indirectly responsible for the crime.

According to widely circulated media accounts, the murders might have been a "hit" in reprisal for human rights activities in which Bishop had been engaged in Ireland.

At the time, Bishop had been an associate with Ter Molen at Mayer, Brown & Platt. A gregarious, willowy blonde with a steel-trap mind, she'd been on the fast track at the firm. But the partners had frowned on the publicity and, reassessing her priorities, she decided to leave.

Since she'd always wanted to practice criminal law and was committed to protecting the rights of the accused, she joined the Cook

County Public Defender's Office, taking a pay cut from $80,000 to $27,000 a year.

The following year, a Winnetka teenager, David Biro, confessed to murdering the Langerts, saying he'd shot them because "they were annoying."

Bishop was relieved that the killer had been caught and that he was too young to be eligible for the death penalty, which she vehemently opposed.

While the trial was pending, Ter Molen contacted her about the Jimerson case, and she readily agreed to help.

Reading the trial transcript, Bishop's thoughts turned to the tragedy in her own family. To her, Carol Schmal and Larry Lionberg were Nancy and Richard Langert—young, happy, planning to spend their lives together, only to be senselessly killed.

Bishop shared the pain of Carol's sister Lynn, who, like her, was the older sister of a murder victim.

And she knew the anguish of William Lionberg and George Schmal, who'd identified their children at the county morgue. Her own father would be forever haunted by the sight of Nancy and Richard in pools of blood on their basement floor.

■ ■ ■

Until the man who'd murdered her sister and brother-in-law was caught, Jeanne Bishop imagined him in a bar somewhere, laughing at news accounts blaming foreign terrorists for the crime.

Bishop now pondered the whereabouts of the real killers of Carol Schmal and Larry Lionberg. Having read the transcripts of the three trials, she was sure they'd gotten away with murder.

Paula Gray's testimony had cinched it for Bishop. The way Gray had answered questions was even more telling than her flip-flops. Her story had been so obviously rehearsed that Bishop thought she might as well have been sitting on a ventriloquist's lap.

Gray had been exquisitely detailed in answering every one of Scott Arthur's questions, repeating the exact language she'd used before the grand jury in 1978. And her curt, vague answers on cross-examination were a sure sign of coaching. She couldn't even remember the deal that would set her free.

The police account of Gray's interrogation also was revealing. Initially, according to Investigator James Houlihan, Gray had implicated Dennis Williams, Kenny Adams, and Willie Rainge, but not Jimerson.

Then Sgt. P. J. Pastirik, the officer who'd arrested Jimerson at the crime scene, took over the questioning. And, at this point, Gray suddenly recalled Jimerson's role.

Had Gray simply forgotten to mention earlier that Jimerson had raped Carol Schmal twice, or had Pastirik put words in her mouth?

To Bishop, the answer was obvious.

How horrible for the incarcerated men and their families. And how tragic for the victims' families, who'd been deceived all these years.

■ ■ ■

Appreciative of Jeanne Bishop's analysis, Mark Ter Molen listed her as cocounsel on the petition for a new trial.

But Ter Molen's strategy was not to attack the state for the wrongful prosecution of *four* men. In fact, he believed the best approach was to *distinguish* his client's case from the others.

Like Bishop, Ter Molen had noted that Paula Gray hadn't named Jimerson when she'd first fingered Dennis Williams, Willie Rainge, and Kenny Adams. That helped only his client.

And Jimerson's alibi wasn't inconsistent with Charles McCraney's claim that he'd seem Jimerson and Williams together a few hours before the murders. Even if McCraney had seen Williams and others run into the abandoned townhouse around 3:00 A.M., that wasn't Jimerson's problem.

Then there was Scott Arthur's failure to tell Jimerson's trial lawyer about the deal with Gray. Great ammunition for Jimerson, but not for Williams and Rainge, whose lawyers had been properly informed.

Ter Molen didn't have to address why Skip Gant and Maurice Scott hadn't cross-examined Gray about the deal. That was irrelevant to Jimerson's case. Ter Molen's task, pure and simple, was to show that Earl Taylor had been ineffective and Scott Arthur unfair.

Besides, Ter Molen sensed from the supreme court opinion in Jimerson's case that the justices had been tentative and equivocal. There even had been a dissent. Not so in the strongly worded unanimous opinions that upheld the convictions of Williams, Rainge, and Adams.

Accordingly, in December of 1991, the Ter Molen team submitted a forty-two-page petition and a six-inch stack of supporting documents to Judge Will Gierach.

They were hoping that Gierach would capriciously deny the petition and that the justices of the Illinois Supreme Court wouldn't fear they were opening a Pandora's box by overruling him.

■ ■ ■

On January 2, 1992, Judge Gierach flatly rejected Verneal Jimerson's plea for a new trial—without holding a hearing.

Citing no case law, Gierach called the petition "frivolous" and "completely without merit."

Mark Ter Molen contacted his client to give him the "good news."

Then he appealed to the Illinois Supreme Court.

■ ■ ■

Dennis Williams, still uncertain in March of 1992 who would handle his final appeals, went to the prison yard to clear his head and seek counsel from Girvies Davis.

Davis wasn't there, so Williams struck up a conversation with another prisoner when, suddenly, he felt disoriented. He lurched, spun around, and collapsed on the concrete, his body convulsing.

After other prisoners screamed for help, two guards arrived with a stretcher. They cuffed Williams and carried him unconscious to the Pit, an area of the prison below Death Row.

When he awoke, the warden and several guards stood over him.

"Buck," said one guard, "do you know who I am?"

"Sergeant Sievers?"

"Yeah," the guard answered. "And what day is it?"

"Wednesday?"

The guard nodded.

"You've had some kind of seizure," said the warden. "We're gonna keep you here and run some tests."

Hours later, after an EEG proved inconclusive, a guard told Williams that the prison was arranging for him to have a CAT scan in the nearby town of Chester.

But first, Williams would spend a night in the Pit, in a dingy cell with only a hard cot and filthy toilet. Alone, listening to vermin scurrying on the floor, he did not sleep.

The next afternoon in Chester, his arms and legs manacled to a hospital table, Williams was slowly enveloped by the huge scanner.

"Please don't move," said the technician, as if that were possible.

Williams, claustrophobic to begin with, was too frightened to laugh.

A doctor arrived later with the results. "There doesn't seem to be anything wrong with you," he said, shrugging. "Just get some rest and you should be fine."

With that, Williams was returned to Death Row. It had been his first experience beyond the walls of Menard since he'd been sentenced to death, for the second time, five years earlier.

■ ■ ■

A worried Girvies Davis greeted Dennis Williams in the prison library.

"Feelin' any better, Buck?" asked Davis.

"Mostly tired, Preacherman," Williams responded. "But it don't matter. I'm gonna die in here, if they don't kill me at Stateville first."

Touching Williams's arm, Davis told him: "I believe the Lord has chosen different paths for us, an' that I'm still around to help you get where you been wantin' to go."

Davis pushed a thick blue book across the table. "Check this out," he said. "It was a gift from my nephew, an' it's got answers for what ails you."

Williams assumed it was a Bible, but, as he looked more closely, saw that it was a medical handbook.

"Look a here," Davis said, opening the book to a section on the side effects of common medications. "Maybe you been takin' too much aspirin."

Davis knew that Williams had recently developed back spasms from bench-pressing weights and had turned to mega-doses of aspirin for relief.

"Preacherman, you might just have something there," said Williams. "I'm goin' off the aspirin straight out. Thanks, bro'."

Williams rose.

"I'll ask the guards to bring this book to your cell," Davis said. "You're gonna need it more than me."

9

A Wake

THURSDAY, MAY 25, 1995

A week and a day after Girvies Davis died by lethal injection, David Protess sat brooding at his desk, the door to his office closed, his head pounding from eight nights of too little sleep and too much scotch.

Chain-smoking Carltons, he gazed endlessly at a snapshot of his student Ryan Owens clasping Davis's manacled hand during their last visit on Death Row.

Protess had arranged grief counseling for Owens and the other students who'd worked on the case, but they seemed to be holding up much better than he was.

He took some comfort from his family and friends, including *Chicago Tribune* columnist Eric Zorn, who'd sent an e-mail message after returning from the execution:

> I don't feel like any of us failed because saving the life of Girvies Davis was not a battle that could have been won. But I think we raised the level of discomfort over the death penalty and gave Girvies the best damn chance he could have had. He went out with a bang, a shooting star across our skies. I think we owe him, as well, for what he gave to us.

Zorn was eager to work on another case involving Protess and his students, but, emotionally, Protess needed a breather.

Then the phone rang.

It was Jeanne Bishop, an old friend, calling with news she knew would lift his spirits: The Illinois Supreme Court had just granted Verneal Jimerson a new trial.

Bishop was gushing as she quoted the choicest parts of the court's unanimous opinion, which, she said, even Mark Ter Molen couldn't have written better.

"The knowing use of perjured testimony constitutes a violation of due process," wrote Chief Justice Michael Bilandic.

Referring to Paula Gray's testimony that prosecutors had promised her nothing, the opinion said: "The state was required to correct this perjured testimony and . . . the failure to do so requires a new trial."

Bilandic found it "particularly disingenuous" that the state had argued on appeal that there had been no deal, when the record clearly showed otherwise. "The justices of the Illinois Supreme Court are not required to suspend common sense in evaluating the evidence in the record," he wrote.

The only troubling part of the opinion was a caveat at the end: "The facts and circumstances of this case are unique. Our holding here is not intended to diminish in any way this court's holding in *People v. Williams*, or the holdings of the appellate court in Rainge's or Adams's appeals."

Bishop faxed Protess a copy of the opinion, which he copied and sent to the students who'd worked on the Girvies Davis case with a cover note:

> Good news—for a change!
>
> The Illinois Supreme Court today reversed Death Row prisoner Verneal Jimerson's murder conviction, and the conclusion about perjured testimony offers a ray of hope for Dennis Williams.

These two guys are as clearly innocent as any I've seen on Death Row. Their case will be my next investigative project.

It's time to reflect on the broader meaning of this development, which is that the system sucks—but not all the time.

■ ■ ■

Grieving over the execution of his best friend, Dennis Williams retaliated by organizing a hunger strike on Death Row.

He'd been studying the life and teachings of Mohandas Gandhi and believed the action would cause consternation among prison officials intent on keeping condemned men healthy enough to kill. (He was now healthy enough, having stopped taking aspirin.)

Sitting cross-legged with his typewriter on his lap, Williams began peppering the news media with letters calling attention to his own "macabre political nightmare."

On May 30, he sent David Protess a thick stack of documents updating the case and imploring him to get involved.

Among the documents was a February 23 order by Judge Frank Meekins summarily denying Williams's petition for a new trial. At Williams's insistence, the petition had included a demand for DNA tests, but Meekins sided with the state.

"Petitioner's allegation that new DNA tests could conclusively prove his innocence is totally unsupported," wrote Meekins.

Another document was an affidavit by David Jackson recanting his 1978 testimony that, while being held at the county jail on burglary charges, he'd overheard Williams and Willie Rainge admit the rape and murders.

In the affidavit, which had recently been obtained by Capital Resource Center investigator Lee Smith, Jackson said he'd lied because he'd been "offered a deal" by prosecutors Scott Arthur and Clifford Johnson.

Jackson added that Arthur "gave me a story to tell as part of the deal." Soon after he'd testified, the prosecutors had dropped the burglary charges and flown him to Minneapolis.

A third document was an affidavit by René Brown summarizing Dennis Johnson's statements about the crime and his offer to testify if prosecutors granted him immunity. Attached were detailed notes of Brown's interviews with Johnson.

Williams's cover letter described the documents as "proof of a conspiracy by the state and its agents to commit murder in the name of Illinois citizens and faithful taxpayers."

As part of the conspiracy, Williams wrote, the supreme court had gone out of its way to distinguish his case from Jimerson's. He saw this as an opening for prosecutors to form an "unholy alliance" with Jimerson, allowing him to go free in exchange for pleading guilty to reduced charges and implicating the others.

"I'm happy for Lurch, but I hope he realizes that he's about to be played off against the rest of us," the letter said.

"Please don't think I'm being paranoid. Girvies was the fifth execution we'd had, and I'm getting closer to the end. The prosecutors taste blood."

■ ■ ■

Unlike Dennis Williams, Rob Warden viewed the Jimerson decision as a terrific opportunity.

Warden, who'd joined the state's attorney's staff in 1994, two years into Jack O'Malley's second term, thought it fortuitous that the original prosecutors were long gone. Clifford Johnson had established a private law practice in 1986, as had Scott Arthur in 1988. Deborah Dooling had become a circuit court judge in 1992.

While their successors also were products of the Markham culture, at least they weren't as personally invested in the case. And O'Malley had instituted sweeping changes at the top of the office.

Most notably, he'd named Andrea Zopp, a former federal prosecutor, as first assistant state's attorney. She was the first African-American and the first woman to hold that position.

Warden, as O'Malley's executive officer, was in the right place to persuade the new blood to take a fresh look at the case.

His strategy was not to argue that all four defendants were innocent and that the office should own up to mistakes spanning seventeen years. That would surely backfire, especially coming from him. Rather, he focused on a way both to help the cause and get the office off the hook in the pending Jimerson case. Since the supreme court had destroyed Paula Gray's last scintilla of credibility, the case looked unwinnable.

Reasoning that it now made sense to agree to DNA testing, Warden drafted a lengthy internal memo reviewing the weakness of the evidence and concluding:

> If [DNA] linked any of the defendants to the semen, it would establish that the prosecution theory of the crime had been correct all along, i.e., the defendants are guilty.
>
> If it linked Jimerson to the crime, it also would make his reconviction a virtual certainty.
>
> If, on the other hand, [DNA] were to exclude all of the defendants as sources of the semen, it could stop a serious miscarriage of justice.

While the memo was making the rounds in the office, Warden surreptitiously shared it with an outsider, someone he'd long wanted to get involved in the case.

■ ■ ■

Perusing the memo, David Protess immediately saw the possibilities.

He could use it to generate media interest in the case and to recruit additional *pro bono* lawyers to take up the cause. It also would be useful background reading for students in his upcoming investigative reporting class.

Protess had a problem, however. The day after Girvies Davis's execution, he'd promised his family that he'd lay off criminal cases for at least six months.

"But you promised Girvies you'd help Dennis," Warden reminded him. "Now's the time."

"Oh, fuck," Protess replied. "Let me copy the memo."

"Just cut the names off the top," said Warden, "and don't divulge the source."

■ ■ ■

Eric Zorn had no trouble guessing the origin of the memo. But since Protess had given it to him "on background," Zorn decided to hold off writing a column until prosecutors decided what to do. He'd blast them for sure, he said, if they opposed DNA testing.

However, WGN-TV's Larry Potash, whose report on Girvies Davis's case had led to the juror recantation, saw an angle for a news story that wouldn't have to mention the memo.

DNA testing, in the summer of 1995, was a matter of intense public interest as a result of the O. J. Simpson trial. The issue raised by the memo, Potash thought, presented an opportunity to put a local spin on a national controversy.

"You've heard about DNA testing during the O. J. Simpson trial," Potash's August 30 story began. "Tonight a special report on how DNA could hold the key in a case right here in Cook County. Dennis Williams has been sitting on Death Row for seventeen years. Now he's hoping this technology will set him free."

A photo of Williams from the 1982 *Chicago Lawyer* story flashed on the screen, as Potash quoted him as saying in a phone interview that Jack O'Malley had an ethical obligation to order the testing.

"If he don't," Williams said in a sound bite, "innocent people are gonna be murdered, and I'll be one of them."

The camera cut to Larry Lionberg's brother saying, "I believe that [Dennis Williams] did do it. As far as the DNA testing is concerned, after so many years, why?"

The piece closed with Protess responding, "If the wrong men are in prison for the murders of their family members, then they're being doubly victimized—by the original killers and by the state in not finding out who those killers are.

"And society is being victimized by the fact that the real killers are on the loose."

Returning live, Potash said the state's attorney's office hadn't yet decided what to do.

■ ■ ■

Mark Ter Molen wasn't pleased by either Rob Warden's memo or Larry Potash's story. In fact, Ter Molen was firmly opposed to DNA testing on behalf of his client.

While he was confident of Verneal Jimerson's innocence, he wasn't so sure about Dennis Williams, Willie Rainge, and Kenny Adams. If DNA implicated even one of them, it would bolster Paula Gray's claim that she'd witnessed the rape. The state could argue that the absence of detectable semen from Jimerson simply meant that he hadn't ejaculated.

Then there was always the possibility of a false positive or, for that matter, that the results would be indefinite and fail to exclude Jimerson.

Ter Molen didn't want to give prosecutors anything they didn't already have, which was nothing.

So he objected when Markham prosecutors, in a classic case of the right hand not knowing what the left was doing, suggested DNA testing. They floated the idea, unaware that the issue was still being debated at the highest levels of the state's attorney's office. When the word finally reached Markham, the prosecutors backed off, which was fine with Ter Molen.

Now Ter Molen only wished David Protess would stop meddling in the matter.

Ter Molen didn't want his client linked with Williams and the others in some cause célèbre. And he didn't want the media pressuring the state's attorney's office for DNA tests.

He just wanted to win in court, as quickly and quietly as possible.

■ ■ ■

In the fall, Larry Potash became a news anchor at WGN-TV, making him unavailable for further investigative reporting on the case.

In need of another television journalist to keep the story going, David Protess turned to Doug Longhini, a local NBC producer who'd worked with him and Rob Warden on the Dowaliby case. Longhini had just returned to channel 5 after a stint at ABC's *Prime Time Live* and was looking for stories.

When Protess pitched the project over lunch, calling it the saga of the "Ford Heights Four," Longhini became excited and said channel 5 had a young African-American reporter, Tracy Haynes, who'd be perfect for the job.

Longhini agreed to assign Haynes to work with Protess and the students from his winter term investigative reporting class. The team would meet to plan strategy in January—after Northwestern returned from its first Rose Bowl appearance in forty-seven years.

■ ■ ■

Wondering what Paula Gray might say if Verneal Jimerson were retried, Mark Ter Molen and Capital Resource Center investigator Appolon Beaudouin paid her a visit.

Gray was now thirty-five, bespectacled, and heavyset. She barely resembled the teenager in the 1982 *Chicago Lawyer* photo.

During a brief conversation in the management office of the Chicago Heights housing complex where she'd recently moved,

Gray stood near the door, arms folded, gazing blankly at the two men.

She didn't respond to most of their questions, but when asked directly whether Verneal Jimerson had taken part in the crime, she replied softly, "I don't remember."

Good enough, Ter Molen thought.

■ ■ ■

Before First Assistant State's Attorney Andrea Zopp was willing to commit to DNA testing, she wanted to take a shot at a simpler way of getting rid of Verneal Jimerson's case: another deal.

If Jimerson would plead guilty, Zopp proposed in November, the state would recommend a sentence that would allow him to be released in seven years or less.

Mark Ter Molen dutifully relayed the offer to his client, who'd been moved to the Cook County Jail. Jimerson laughed. "Tell them to go scratch themselves," he said.

Ter Molen told prosecutors the offer wasn't acceptable and suggested, "Why don't you let him go now?"

As Christmas approached, Zopp agreed that Jimerson could walk without further ado if he'd confess to the crime.

That was an offer Jimerson had to seriously consider.

■ ■ ■

Verneal Jimerson hadn't felt such agony since he'd been sentenced to die ten Christmases ago.

He could taste freedom. All he had to do was sign a few papers, say the right words, and he'd go home to his family.

But he'd be admitting to being the killer he wasn't, and any chance for Dennis Williams and the others would be gone.

Deeply troubled, he turned daily to Sister Miriam Wilson, a jail chaplain and leader of the Illinois Coalition Against the Death Penalty. She'd often visited him on Death Row, and he found her a source of comfort and guidance.

After listening as Jimerson wrestled with his dilemma, Sister Miriam gently reminded him of the eighth commandment: "Thou shalt not bear false witness against thy neighbor."

But she reassured him that God would love him no matter what he decided.

He also sought the counsel of Jeanne Bishop, asking her, "What would you do if you were in my shoes?"

Bishop wanted him to reject the deal, but thought she shouldn't say so. What for her was a matter of principle was for him a matter of life and death.

"You're the one who's got to go back to that cell," she told him. "Only you can decide what's best for you and what you can handle."

Mark Ter Molen expressed the same sentiment. Ever cautious, however, he wouldn't be unhappy if Jimerson said yes and avoided rolling the dice with another jury.

Only Jimerson's family members said in no uncertain terms that he should stay strong and reject the deal. They believed it was immoral for prosecutors to suggest that he confess to a crime he didn't commit. But seeing his family made him want to rejoin them as soon as possible.

Alone in his cell, shortly before New Year's, Jimerson made his decision—no deal.

And he wanted DNA testing to exonerate him once and for all.

"You're the bravest man I know," said Ter Molen.

10

Class Actions

■ "Welcome to Investigative Journalism," David Protess told sixteen Medill seniors on January 3, 1996. "In this class, we'll be investigating real-world miscarriages of justice.

"There's no way to know how many wrongful convictions there are, but even if the error rate in the criminal justice system were only one percent there'd be more than ten thousand cases in the country. In the months ahead, we'll look into four different Illinois cases that may well fall into this category."

The class, Protess explained, would be divided into investigative teams. Each student could express a preference for a case and, unless too many picked the same one, he'd go along with their choices.

Protess wrote the names of the cases on a chalkboard and summarized the facts of each, pacing as he spoke. He saved the Ford Heights Four case for last, saying it was the one in which he would be most directly involved.

"If you choose this case," he warned, "be prepared to go into some rough neighborhoods, and to Death Row."

He also cautioned them about the emotional danger of getting too close to condemned prisoners, citing the experience of the previous year's class with Girvies Davis.

"But there's a chance, if your reporting is thorough, that you'll make a difference in the lives of four men who I think are innocent," he said.

When he asked for an initial expression of preference, four hands shot up for the Ford Heights Four.

Two of the hands belonged to Laura Sullivan and Stephanie Goldstein, both of whom had been in Protess's Law and Ethics of Journalism class the previous term.

Sullivan, the daughter of a San Francisco lawyer, was gutsy, outspoken, and, Protess thought, well suited for the tough interviews that would be required.

Goldstein, a native of Birmingham and the stepdaughter of a judge, was polite, brainy, and capable of mastering the massive case files.

Protess didn't know the others personally, but he'd heard about them through the faculty grapevine.

Stacey Delo, whose parents were St. Louis business executives, had been described as sweet and empathetic, a "people person." For interviewing, she seemed like a perfect partner for Laura Sullivan.

Christe Guidibaldi, the daughter of a Cleveland lawyer, was said to be bright and hardworking. Her time was limited because she was working to earn money for law school, but she could pitch in with the interviewing and help the team get a handle on the paper trail.

It was fortunate, Protess believed, that female students had chosen the project, since the first witness he planned to have them interview was a very guarded woman—Paula Gray.

■ ■ ■

That same day, Judge Sheila Murphy was grappling with a decision that she feared might end her judicial career.

As the presiding judge in the Markham district, she was entertaining a motion by Mark Ter Molen to set bond for Verneal Jimerson.

If she granted the motion, Jimerson would be released until his case was resolved.

Granting bond in any amount to a defendant still facing the death penalty was unprecedented in Illinois, but, in addition to that, Ter Molen was asking her to require his client to post only what the family could afford: $2,500.

Behind the prosecutors, who opposed any bond, was a legion of spectators wearing green and white badges that the state's attorney's office usually provided to witnesses. When Murphy inquired about the group, prosecutor Robert Milan said they were family and friends of Carol Schmal and Larry Lionberg. And with them, Murphy noticed, was Scott Arthur.

The media, of course, were present, and Murphy could imagine the headlines if she let Jimerson out on bond and he committed a crime.

Well, she'd asked for it by assigning the case to herself after the supreme court remanded it for a new trial. It was a "heater" case and, as presiding judge, she felt an obligation to take the heat, even though she'd have to face the voters in less than three years.

But Sheila Murphy hadn't gotten this far by letting politics get in her way. A former assistant public defender, she'd won election to the bench by running with an independent slate of women who challenged the old-boy network that controlled political slate-making.

When she was named presiding judge in Markham, where she'd been a defense lawyer in two capital cases (saving both clients from death sentences), she mused that "God certainly has a sense of humor."

In fact, the humorless chief judge of the circuit court, Harry Comerford, had given her the job in 1992 to mute criticism that the bench was overwhelmingly dominated by men who were former prosecutors. (Her immediate predecessor had been none other than Frank Meekins.)

Since her appointment, she'd launched several innovative programs, including alternative sentencing for drug offenders, confidential HIV testing, and a supervised playroom with free lunches for children who accompanied their parents to court. To brighten the atmosphere, she'd had flowers planted and personally patrolled the grounds for litter.

Now, at age fifty-eight, the petite, auburn-haired jurist was ready to tackle a case that represented a historic challenge to the Markham establishment. And she was determined to base her decision on the facts and the law, whatever the consequences.

After the arguments for and against bond for Jimerson, she retired to her spacious chambers on the second floor of the courthouse to review the evidence.

She'd heard the prosecution promise that Gray would testify exactly as she had at Jimerson's 1985 trial. "I believe that you will find her credible, or a jury will find her credible," Milan said. But Apolon Beaudouin, the investigator who'd gone with Ter Molen to interview Gray, had testified that Gray said she "didn't remember" whether Jimerson had participated in the crime.

To Murphy, it was yet another conflict over what Gray might say. On top of the supreme court's attack on Gray's previous testimony, she simply wasn't a strong enough witness to justify denying bond. And the prosecution had offered nothing else.

Moreover, Ter Molen had presented evidence that Jimerson had strong roots in the community and was unlikely to flee.

The conclusion that Jimerson was entitled to a reasonable bond seemed inescapable. The remaining question was how to define "reasonable." Requiring more than the Jimerson family could afford would be the same as denying bond, which Murphy thought was unreasonable.

She returned to the courtroom, took her seat behind the bench, and gazed at the spectators.

"The only testimony that is holding Mr. Verneal Jimerson at this time is the testimony of Paula Gray," Murphy said.

"When Paula Gray was sworn to tell the truth, she did not tell the truth. And to compound the error, the state's attorney's office did not correct her when she lied to the jury.

"The proof here is not evident and the presumption [necessary to deny bond] is not great."

Accordingly, Murphy set bond in the amount requested by Ter Molen.

There were loud groans from the Schmal and Lionberg contingent and a mixture of smiles and tears from a small group of African-Americans sitting behind Ter Molen and Jimerson.

Murphy adjourned court, suppressing a smile of her own.

■ ■ ■

When Sheila Murphy arrived at her chambers the morning of January 12, she found a copy of an editorial from a south suburban community newspaper, *The Star*, blasting her decision.

"A bitter pill," the headline said.

"Perhaps Judge Sheila Murphy knows something that isn't readily apparent to the rest of us," read the text. "Murphy must have some reason for releasing convicted murderer Verneal Jimerson on a surprisingly low bond. . . .

"The Lionberg-Schmal abduction-murder case was a horrific experience for the southern suburbs. It was devastating to the victims' families and close friends. . . .

"[Murphy's] choice is tough to swallow."

While Murphy took the editorial in stride, she told aides she was troubled by the manner in which it had come to her attention: Someone had dropped it anonymously at the door of her chambers, an area accessible only to prosecutors, judges, and court personnel.

■ ■ ■

Verneal Jimerson's release prompted Eric Zorn to weigh in with a *Tribune* column headlined, "How yet another flimsy case ended up on Death Row."

Zorn called Sheila Murphy's decision "a strong signal to all concerned—particularly Cook County State's Attorney Jack O'Malley, who inherited this prosecution—that the case is insubstantial and ought to be dropped. . . .

"The next step is to provide comfort to the victims' families, who deserve to know what actually happened and to see real justice done."

■ ■ ■

For Mark Ter Molen, the timing of Eric Zorn's column couldn't have been worse.

The morning it appeared, Ter Molen met with State's Attorney Jack O'Malley and First Assistant Andrea Zopp to discuss their next step in the case.

They gave him a chilly reception, assuming, incorrectly, that he'd orchestrated the publicity.

The case wouldn't be dropped, they said.

Just because Paula Gray had lied about the deal didn't mean she was lying about witnessing the crime; she knew too many accurate details for her not to have been there.

Ter Molen tried to argue, but got nowhere.

When he asked about DNA testing, they said the state's attorney's office would oppose it, but didn't say why.

Thinking the prosecutors might only be posturing, Ter Molen left the meeting intent on keeping the state's latest position to himself.

He didn't need another Zorn column that might cause O'Malley and Zopp to dig in their heels.

■ ■ ■

Dennis Williams had authorized David Protess's students to review the Capital Resource Center's files on his case, hoping to meet them when they finished.

But, only two weeks into the new school term, Williams called Protess in a panic, asking to see the students right away concerning an urgent matter that he didn't want to discuss on the phone.

"It's a red alert," he said.

Although Protess had intended to put off a face-to-face meeting until the students were sufficiently steeped in the case to conduct a meaningful interview, Williams's concern—whatever it was—seemed to warrant a change in the agenda.

And Protess thought it made sense for the students to see Kenny Adams on the same trip. He'd been granted a transfer to a medium-security prison in Danville, which was on the way to Menard.

After arranging the interviews with the Department of Corrections, Protess took the four students to dinner at a favorite haunt, the Roxy Cafe in Evanston, where he briefed them on prison rules and primed them to ask questions he still had about the case.

On January 15, at daybreak, the students hit the road.

■ ■ ■

"Do you know what this guy's in here for?" a guard asked the four young women when they arrived at the Danville Correctional Center.

They knew, but the query heightened their trepidation about entering a room alone with a convicted rapist and murderer.

Then they met Kenny Adams.

Charismatic, handsome, and polite, he spoke with a quiet dignity that quickly put them at ease.

He reported that he'd had other visitors just minutes earlier—two investigators from the state's attorney's office.

The investigators wanted to make a deal to reduce his sentence if he'd testify against Verneal Jimerson, but he'd cut the discussion short and asked them to leave.

It was the fifth such overture he'd had from the state's attorney's office in the eighteen-year course of the case, he said. At this point, he didn't care to hear anything prosecutors or their emissaries had to say, short of an apology for ruining his life.

Since his arrival at Danville in 1988, he'd become a teacher's aide and taken up woodworking. He'd made oak cabinets, compact-disk cases, and chess sets for his family. For the Danville chapel, he'd built a podium that had been appropriated for a purpose he didn't appreciate: Governor Jim Edgar had stood behind it to dedicate a new prison.

When Stacey Delo asked if he had a message for Paula Gray, whom the students hoped to see soon, he said he wanted her to know he felt no bitterness. "She was weak, and the cops took advantage of her," he said. "As far as I'm concerned, she's just another victim."

Laura Sullivan asked about his alibi for the night of the crime. He said it was true that he'd been at the Gray home with Paula. She'd braided his hair and they'd listened to Barry White love songs in his car. Then Dennis Williams had driven by and they'd talked for a while. A little later, shortly after midnight, Paula had gone inside and he'd gone home to bed.

"Would you be willing to submit to DNA testing to prove you didn't rape Carol Schmal?" Sullivan asked.

"I've wanted that for years," he replied.

"But you're an A secretor," she said, "same as one of the rapists."

"The tests will prove I didn't do it," he predicted.

When the visit ended, Adams firmly shook the students' hands, thanked them for coming, and invited them to write or return if they had more questions.

As the guards led him away, he turned and smiled.

Outside the prison, Goldstein burst into tears.

"I can't believe a man like that is in this place," she said, as Delo consoled her.

"I don't know," Sullivan muttered. "He could be conning us."

■ ■ ■

After spending the night at the home of Stacey Delo's parents in Ladue, the poshest suburb of St. Louis, the students crossed the Mississippi River and headed for Death Row at Menard.

Dennis Williams was handcuffed and hobbled by leg irons as a guard led him to a Formica table in the dank visiting room where the four young women awaited him. His breast pocket contained toothpicks, which he chewed to avoid smoking in front of them.

"It's okay, Mr. Williams, if you want to smoke," Delo assured him.

Impressed by her intuitiveness, he laughed and lit up.

He hadn't had visitors in quite some time, and never any who looked quite like these women. Stacey, tall, slender, with strawberry-blond hair and hazel eyes, was a raving beauty, he thought. The others were fine, too—Laura Sullivan, a cream-complected blonde; Christe Guidibaldi, a high-cheekboned brunette; and Stephanie Goldstein, a big-eyed redhead with long, curly locks.

It wasn't easy, under the circumstances, to summon the outrage with which he'd intended to describe his latest legal trauma, so at first he rambled generally about the criminal justice system.

Asked about his teenage encounter with the system, he readily acknowledged stealing a motorcycle. When caught, he'd been charged both with theft and with torching a vacant building. Although he knew nothing of the arson, he said, prosecutors had offered him a lenient sentence if he'd plead guilty to both crimes, so he took the package deal.

The experience had left him cynical about law-enforcement officials "who cared more about doin' a deal than who did the crime" and he'd sworn never again to confess to something he didn't do. That vow had given him strength the night he'd been interrogated at gunpoint about the murders of Larry Lionberg and Carol Schmal.

Sullivan questioned him at length about his whereabouts on the night of May 10–11, 1978, eliciting an account consistent with his previous statements.

When Sullivan asked why he'd been in the crowd the morning of May 12, Williams said he'd promised to take Paula Gray's mother shopping and, upon arriving, had seen the police and people milling around.

"Like everybody else, I was just curious," he said. "Do you think I'd be stupid enough to go to a place where I'd just committed two murders?"

An hour into the interview, Williams raised the matter that had prompted his urgent call to David Protess: He'd received a letter from his Capital Resource Center attorney, John Greenlees, warning that Verneal Jimerson might be seriously contemplating cutting a deal with the state.

Although the letter had arrived the day Williams called, it had been written three weeks earlier but was delayed because the wrong prisoner ID number was on the envelope.

Williams was worried that, by now, his worst fear might already be a reality: Jimerson might have falsely corroborated Paula Gray's story in exchange for his freedom.

"It is of the utmost imperative," Williams told the students, "to have your professor check this out and, if the deal has not been done, to head it off with media publicity."

The students, knowing nothing about any deal for Jimerson, promised to relay the message.

Williams appreciated that, and asked the students to make one more request of Protess: to please help him find another lawyer.

■ ■ ■

As the students filled in David Protess over calzone at the Roxy Cafe, Stephanie Goldstein asked, "Is Dennis Williams being paranoid?"

"Well, the state *is* trying to kill him," said Protess. "But his lawyer is messing up his mind by not keeping him informed. Jimerson's already rejected the deal."

Finding Williams a new lawyer would be a priority.

But Protess had a different concern.

"Does it strike anyone as curious that the state showed up at Danville just before you saw Kenny Adams?" he asked.

"Now *you're* being paranoid," said Laura Sullivan.

"Maybe," said Protess. "Maybe not."

■ ■ ■

Ghetto 101: That's how Paul Ciolino characterized a briefing he'd been giving for years to prepare David Protess's upscale students to conduct interviews in downscale neighborhoods.

Ciolino, a street-smart private detective who'd worked with Protess and Rob Warden on several cases, always began by discussing safety ("Go before the gang-bangers wake up and wear running shoes") and ways to get a foot in the door ("Say that you've only got one quick question or that your grade depends on them talking to you").

After his lecture, the students role-played an interview, which Ciolino critiqued. Today, Laura Sullivan was Paula Gray, and Stephanie Goldstein the principal interviewer.

Sullivan stood silently with her arms folded, while Goldstein tried to break the ice by relaying the message from Kenny Adams.

When Sullivan didn't react, Ciolino suggested a different tack: "Empathize with what *she's* gone through."

"I can't imagine the strain you've been under all these years," Goldstein resumed.

"Yeah, I guess." Sullivan shrugged.

"Look," Ciolino told Goldstein, "Paula's probably most concerned about perjury. So if she's about to slam the door in your face, say your professor knows a way that she can tell the truth without getting in trouble."

"And I'll come down the next day," Protess chimed in.

Ciolino had one more bit of advice: "Take a tape recorder in case she opens up—and check the batteries."

■ ■ ■

To help open the door, David Protess wrote Paula Gray a letter on Northwestern letterhead saying his students had seen Kenny Adams, who didn't blame her for what had happened.

The letter added that Adams had a message for her that the students would soon deliver in person.

On February 7, Laura Sullivan, Stephanie Goldstein, and Stacey Delo knocked on Paula Gray's door.

When Gray found out who they were, she let them in right away.

The two-bedroom apartment was immaculate. A velvet portrait of Jesus adorned the living room wall above an overstuffed couch where Gray invited the students to sit. On the coffee table were framed photos of several children.

Asked about the children, Gray said they were hers. She'd had six by a boyfriend she met soon after her release, but they'd been taken away by the state "because of this case."

"Kenny asked us to tell you he considers you a victim, just like him," Goldstein said. "He knows the last eighteen years have been a nightmare for you, too."

"I still love Kenny," Gray said. "I wish my babies was his."

"Do you want us to tell him that?" Sullivan asked.

"Uh-huh," she said, "and tell him I'm sorry."

"Sorry for what?"

Gray sat silently for what seemed like an eternity before saying, "For lyin' on him and the others. We never hurt no white people."

Sullivan asked if Gray would be willing to talk on tape, and without giving her a chance to say no, placed the recorder on an end table near her.

Gray spoke as if she were in a trance, repeating that she and the four men were innocent and claiming police and prosecutors had forced her to lie. But asked specifically how she'd been forced, Gray clammed up.

Finally, she said she feared "getting in more trouble," claiming that prosecutor Robert Milan had ordered her not to talk about the case or "he'll lock me up and I'll never get my kids back."

Delo suggested that she meet with their professor, who would try to prevent that from happening.

Gray nodded and escorted the students to the door.

"Thank you for seeing us, Paula," Goldstein said.

"Thank *you* for comin'," Gray replied.

■ ■ ■

Alone in her apartment, Paula Gray recalled a dream she'd had the very night before: Several young white women had come knocking on her door to talk about the case. As soon as she saw them, she knew it was time to let the truth be told.

Lord, that dream had been prophetic.

■ ■ ■

Laura Sullivan called David Protess from her car phone.

She was ecstatic—until she tried to play the tape of Paula Gray's interview.

The batteries worked. That wasn't the problem. She'd placed the recorder too close to a forced-air heat duct.

The conversation was drowned out by a loud whooshing.

Protess was peeved.

"If she denies everything," he sputtered, "it's your word against hers."

He asked Sullivan to call Gray and invite her to dinner at a restaurant the following night.

A few minutes later, a very relieved Laura Sullivan called back to say it was all arranged.

■ ■ ■

The next morning, over the phone from the state's attorney's office, Rob Warden helped David Protess draft an affidavit they hoped Paula Gray would sign.

The affidavit included statements Gray had made in her original recantation in 1978 and relevant comments she'd made to the students.

After running the language past Mark Ter Molen, who offered additional suggestions, Protess printed the document and set out in a blinding snowstorm to rendezvous with Gray and the students.

A hostess seated the group at a round table in the rear of Venice Restaurant, a half a mile from Gray's home. "I've never been here before," Gray said, smiling broadly. As a matter of fact, she added, this would be her first dinner out since her release from prison nine years before. She ordered a full slab of ribs, corn on the cob, and a large Coke.

The conversation was relaxed but to the point.

Protess explained that if she told the truth, it might help Kenny Adams and the others come home. And if she told her story publicly through the media, it was unlikely that she'd be prosecuted for perjury. But if that happened, Protess would find her a lawyer.

"I believe God sent y'all so I could lift this burden off my soul," Gray said.

Protess went over the affidavit line by line.

"That's true," she said each time he paused. She agreed that after dinner she'd sign it in front of a notary.

Then Protess leaned forward, looked her straight in the eye, and asked, "Paula, if you weren't there, how'd you know so much about the crime?"

Tears filled Gray's eyes. As Protess and the students scribbled notes, she described the interrogation that led to her false statements.

"Five or six white cops, all in plain clothes, took me over to the place, Cannon Lane." she said. "They yells at me, 'This is where the lady got killed, this is where you walked her up the steps in the middle of the night, and you had a Bic lighter.' The cops made up the lighter. I did smoke, but I didn't have no lighter.

"They kept yellin', 'This is where she got raped and killed—Dennis shot her twice in the head, didn't he?' I seen the blood on the floor, a lot of blood, and they showed me some clothes and said they was the lady's. Then one of 'em screams, 'You know that they raped her. You saw Dennis shoot her in the head, didn't you? *Didn't you?*'

"I kept sayin' everything's a lie, but I'm so scared I don't know what to do. I'm like a zombie. All of a sudden, I just start answering, 'Yes, yes, yes.'

"They take me outside by the creek with flashlights. They says, 'Dennis shot the man in the head. Willie shot him in the back, too, didn't he?' 'Yes, yes,' I says.

"They says they found the gun in the creek with Dennis's fingerprints on it. Then they asks, 'Well, what about the gun?' an' I jus' tells 'em, 'Dennis threw it in the creek.'

"They says, 'Dennis threatened you, didn't he?' I says, 'No, Dennis ain't like that.' But they takes me to a motel an' says, 'The same thing that happened to the lady, it will happen to you.' I thought they was gonna rape me, an' I lock myself in the bathroom."

Gray paused and her eyes became glassy. She recalled nothing else about the interrogation at the motel, and her memory was hazy about testifying before the grand jury and being hospitalized a couple of days later.

Protess turned on a tape recorder and she repeated the gist of what she'd just said. When she finished, he offered to record a message to play for the four men she'd put in prison.

"I'm sorry for what I did to you all," she said. "Kenny, I still love you. I think about you all the time. An' Dennis, I heard about your mamma dyin'. I'm sorry. I remember all the fun times we had, and I miss you. I hope you'll forgive me."

■ ■ ■

When David Protess dropped Paula Gray off at her apartment after she'd signed the affidavit, he noticed, out of the corner of his eye, a man sitting behind the wheel of a light-colored, late-model car.

Odd, he thought, that someone would be parked in front of a housing project, late at night, during a snowstorm.

Protess looked at the man, who quickly turned his head.

It was probably nothing.

Putting it out of his mind, for the moment, Protess joined the students at a sports bar to celebrate.

■ ■ ■

Paula Gray sounded hysterical when she called David Protess the next morning.

"They know I talked to y'all."

"Who knows?"

"Bob Milan, the prosecutor. He just called me and says he's sending some men over to bring me in."

"Damn," said Protess, thinking of the car he'd noticed the previous night. "What'd you tell him?"

"That I wasn't gonna talk to him no more."

Gray said she'd slammed down the phone and was thinking about "hidin' out somewhere."

"Go to a safe place—don't say where over the phone—and call me later," Protess advised.

He immediately called Eric Zorn, filling him in on Gray's recantation and Milan's reaction.

Zorn in turn called Milan, who became flustered when asked why he'd just contacted Paula Gray.

Stumbling for an answer, he finally said, "Hey, I don't have to talk to you."

■ ■ ■

Paula Gray did not hide out.

Her anger had overcome her fear, and she'd stayed home, ready to confront Robert Milan's men.

But they hadn't shown up.

"I'll be waitin' if they come," she vowed to David Protess. "I ain't afraid to tell the truth, an' I ain't runnin' from nobody no more."

11

In Search of Salvation

▪ It wasn't much fun, sitting on the floor of the Capital Resource Center's file room, drowning in documents.

Surrounding Laura Sullivan and Christe Guidibaldi were seven huge boxes jammed with every scrap of paper generated over eighteen years in Dennis Williams's case, twenty or thirty thousand pages.

Their main assignment was to find one document: notes of an interview that had taken place in 1978 at St. James Hospital in Chicago Heights.

The task would have been daunting under any circumstances, but the files were a mess, in no particular order. And the students didn't know who'd conducted the interview, who'd been interviewed, or the subject matter discussed.

All they knew was that Willie Rainge had somehow heard that it could be important, that it might be in the Williams file, and that their professor had assigned them to look for it.

Rainge, it seemed to the students, was on a fishing expedition, hoping to find new evidence for a hearing the appellate court had ordered in his case after Verneal Jimerson won a new trial.

Since Rainge was currently between lawyers, he was relying on David Protess, and by extension them, for research a lawyer should be doing.

So there they were, on the floor, one box to go.

Then, near the bottom of that box, in an envelope, Sullivan hit pay dirt—a copy of a three-page, hand-printed report of an interview by three police officers with a man named Marvin Simpson at St. James Hospital. The interview had taken place on May 17, 1978, five days after Larry Lionberg and Carol Schmal were found dead.

The first thing that jumped out was that Simpson had named four "suspects" from East Chicago Heights who'd been talking about "doing a score, a stickup" on the night the victims were kidnapped.

Although the students didn't recognize the names of any of the suspects, they were certainly familiar with two of the officers present at the interview: Howard Vanick, who'd led the sheriff's investigation, and David Capelli, who'd arrested Dennis Williams and Verneal Jimerson.

The report didn't mention a Clark station or Lionberg and Schmal, but it quoted Simpson as saying one of the suspects "got real scared and panicky" when a body was found beside Deer Creek on May 12.

And, the report said, Simpson had seen the suspects in a Buick Electra 225—armed with a .38.

■ ■ ■

Laura Sullivan strode into David Protess's office, document in hand, the other three students in tow.

Protess didn't have to read far before he leaped to his feet. "Holy shit!" he exclaimed as his eyes darted over the names listed under the heading "Suspects."

Suspect number one, he told the startled students, was a man whose name had appeared prominently in René Brown's affidavit and notes: Dennis Johnson, the Dude.

And the other suspects almost certainly were the men Johnson had mentioned in his conversations with Brown:

- Arthur Robinson, nicknamed Red, the report said.
- Juan Rodriguez, nicknamed Johnny, and, according to the report, the owner of the Buick Electra 225, a deuce and a quarter.
- Ira Johnson, Dennis's younger brother, who the report said had owned a .38 and "panicked" when Larry Lionberg's body was discovered. Ira might well be the "friend" Dennis swore he'd never implicate.

Just as amazing, the cops—Howard Vanick, David Capelli, and a "Lt. Nance, East Chicago Heights PD"—had known about the alternative suspects almost right from the start.

"It's a goddamn street file," Protess said, waving the document. "Police notes that probably weren't meant to see the light of day."

"Then why was it with Dennis Williams's stuff?" Sullivan asked.

"Good question," Protess responded. "And how did it get there, and when? Suddenly there are a lot of questions we need answered."

Thinking out loud, Protess wondered if the cops had investigated Marvin Simpson's lead and concluded there was nothing to it. But if so, where were the follow-up reports of their investigation? Had the cops, for some reason, done nothing with the lead, even though they'd gotten it within a week of the crime? And why hadn't the defense acted on it?

Protess said he'd contact the Capital Resource Center to see if they had answers, and try to locate Vanick, Capelli, and Lieutenant Nance. And Paul Ciolino, the private investigator who'd taught the students how to break the ice with Paula Gray, was just the guy to track down Marvin Simpson.

"What do *we* get to do?" Sullivan demanded.

"Well, where would you first look for suspects like these four guys?" Protess asked.

"I'll call the Department of Corrections to see if they're in prison," Stephanie Goldstein suggested.

"If you find them," Protess promised, "you'll get first crack at the interviews."

■ ■ ■

Although the street file had been buried in mounds of documents at the Capital Resource Center, it hadn't escaped the attention of the agency's lawyers and investigators.

John Greenlees, Dennis Williams's lawyer, told David Protess he'd found the report in the boxes that had been lugged to the Center by Williams's previous legal team.

From a note attached to the report—"Found in Skip's files"—Greenlees surmised that prosecutors had finally turned it over to Skip Gant prior to Williams's retrial. That made sense, Greenlees reasoned, because it wasn't until 1983 that the courts began requiring police to disclose street files when subpoenaed by defense lawyers. However, there was nothing to indicate that Gant, who was distracted by his own legal problems at the time of the retrial, had even read the report.

Since taking over the case, Greenlees said, he'd tried to figure out which of the cops had penned the street file and to contact the alternative suspects, but to no avail. He'd suspended these efforts to focus on matters that he considered more pressing, including Williams's petition for a new trial, which the Illinois Supreme Court was about to consider.

The only solid lead on the street file had been developed by Verneal Jimerson's Capital Resource Center investigator, Appolon Beaudouin. He'd found Lieutenant Nance, George Nance, now retired. Beaudouin had spoken briefly with Nance, who was willing to discuss the case, but Beaudouin hadn't followed up because he'd been consumed with interviewing witnesses expected to be called at

Jimerson's forthcoming trial. He was pleased to provide Protess with Nance's address and unlisted phone number.

The other cops named in the street file, Howard Vanick and David Capelli, were still employed by the sheriff's police and wouldn't talk to Beaudouin.

Marvin Simpson hadn't been found.

And, of the four suspects, Beaudouin was sure of the whereabouts of only one: Dennis Johnson.

The Dude was dead.

■ ■ ■

"It's true," Rob Warden told David Protess. "Dennis Johnson died in Minneapolis, maybe four or five years ago."

Warden related that Johnson's body had been found in the backseat of his car, which doubled as his residence. There had been no evidence of foul play. The autopsy indicated he'd died of an abdominal hemorrhage, and cocaine had been found in his system.

Since Johnson had taken the identities of the other suspects to his grave, Warden had lost hope that the crime would ever be solved. In light of the discovery of the street file, however, he thought Johnson's death might actually help the investigation.

"Now that you've got names attached to the suspects, they just might talk if you can find them," he said. "Confront them with the street file and maybe they'll try to get off the hook by blaming the dead guy."

■ ■ ■

It didn't take long to locate Ira Johnson. He was at the Menard Correctional Center, Stephanie Goldstein learned.

And Johnson, now thirty-six, would be staying put for quite some time. In 1991, he'd been sentenced to seventy-four years for first-degree murder.

Johnson had confessed to killing thirty-one-year-old Cherry Wilder in an apparent dispute over drugs, court documents showed. He'd dragged the young African-American woman into an abandoned apartment in Chicago Heights, where he strangled her with a rope and suffocated her with a plastic bag.

The crime was horrible enough, Goldstein thought, but it was even worse to contemplate that Ira Johnson might be a triple murderer and that Cherry Wilder might still be alive if the authorities had done their job in 1978.

This class project was getting a bit too unsettling for Goldstein, who told David Protess she'd just as soon not have first dibs on interviewing Ira. Perhaps she could simply continue the search for Red Robinson and Johnny Rodriguez, neither of whom had turned up in the check of prison records.

That was okay with Protess and, since Christe Guidibaldi had almost no time left to work on the case, he offered the interview to Laura Sullivan and Stacey Delo. They were ready to go—as long as they didn't have to tell Johnson their last names or addresses, at least for now.

To facilitate the interview, Protess wrote Johnson a letter saying two of his students, "Laura" and "Stacey," would like to see him.

"They want to talk to you about your case . . . and share some information concerning your brother Dennis and a man you may know named Marvin Simpson," said the letter, which invited him to call collect.

A few days later, Johnson's sister Jackie called. "Is this about Tuna and them boys?" she demanded.

"Who's Tuna?" Protess responded, as if he didn't know.

"If you don't know I ain't gonna tell you," she said. "Our family's been through enough and we don't want no more trouble."

"Yeah, I heard about your brother Dennis. I'm sorry."

"Ain't your fault. Man was messin' with drugs, always into bad shit. But Ira, he didn't do no murder."

"If he's innocent, maybe we can help him. Will you have him call me?"

"Ira gets hisself in trouble runnin' his mouth." She hesitated. "I don't want him talking to you, but it's his life. Probably can't fuck it up no worse than he 'ready has."

■ ■ ■

While Ira Johnson was taking his time deciding whether to see the students, private investigator Paul Ciolino began in earnest to look for the man who'd first provided the lead on Johnson and the others eighteen years earlier, Marvin Simpson.

Using computer databases to search the southern suburbs, Ciolino found a Marvin Simpson listed in an African-American section of Markham. He was born in 1954, the year of Simpson's birth, as noted in the street file.

Ciolino and David Protess drove down to see him. As they approached the white frame house, a decidedly unfriendly rottweiler bounded toward them, stopped only by a chain-link fence.

"You think he can jump that fence?" Protess asked.

"I don't think we wanna find out," said Ciolino.

They backed away and went next door, introducing themselves to a man who was struggling to get a Harley-Davidson motorcycle out of his basement. The neighbor agreed to talk, if Ciolino and Protess helped him complete the chore.

"I know the Simpsons," the man finally told his out-of-breath visitors. "Real tragic."

Marvin Simpson, he explained, had recently died of a self-inflicted gunshot wound.

"Shit," Protess said, more upset about the likely loss of a key source than the tragedy of the suicide.

Giving the neighbor a business card, Ciolino asked him to pass it along to Marvin Simpson's widow, hoping that she'd contact him with further information.

That night, Loretta Simpson called. She said her husband had been depressed for many years about "things he wouldn't discuss."

Ciolino asked if he'd ever mentioned knowing anything about the 1978 murders in East Chicago Heights.

"No, but he did live around there when he was younger," she said.

In the year or so before his death, she added hesitatingly, he'd admitted having an ongoing affair with a woman "somewhere in the Heights."

"I didn't know her name," she said, "but he was there all the time."

■ ■ ■

With Marvin Simpson presumed dead, David Protess wanted to make a quick trip to Ford Heights to check out a lead on Red Robinson. Capital Resource Center investigator Appolon Beaudouin had provided the address of a Robinson family he thought might be related to Red.

Believing there would be safety in numbers and curious to see the town, Stephanie Goldstein and Stacey Delo decided to go along at the last minute.

Their arrival at the address, Protess in a brand-new Infiniti and the students in Delo's turbocharged Volvo, drew intense stares from neighbors. "Let's not stick around any longer than necessary," said Protess.

As he and the students approached the house, a young woman stepped outside. "Does Red Robinson live here?" Protess asked.

"No," the woman answered.

"Do you know where he lives?"

"You might check across the street," she said, pointing to a dilapidated house.

Protess knocked on the door and moved to the side, telling the students to stand back for safety's sake. But before they could budge, a disheveled, glassy-eyed man swung the door open.

"Red?" Protess asked after several moments of mutual staring.

The man beckoned them inside.

" 'Scuze me, got something cooking on the stove," said the man, retreating to the kitchen where two zombielike persons leaned against a wall.

Protess stopped in his tracks, knowing a crack house when he saw one. "Uh, we'll wait outside," he said, pushing the students out the door.

The man soon returned, and Protess asked, "Are you Red Robinson?"

Without answering, the man pointed to the house across the street where they'd just been.

"Does he live *there*?"

"Used to."

With that, the man walked back inside and closed the door.

By now, a group had gathered on the street, eyeing the strangers and their cars.

"Enough for today," Protess told the students. "Back to Evanston."

■ ■ ■

On February 12, Eric Zorn was pushing deadline for a *Tribune* column about Paula Gray, who'd repeated her recantation to him.

Convinced that Gray now was telling the truth, he wanted to find out why the cops had continued to believe her original story after they'd talked to Marvin Simpson.

The only person likely to shed light on that question, Zorn thought, was George Nance. So Zorn interrupted his writing to call the retired East Chicago Heights police officer, whose number he'd obtained from David Protess.

The interview exceeded Zorn's expectations.

Nance said he'd always been suspicious of Paula Gray's story, and Charles McCraney's.

"I interviewed him first at the crime scene," Nance said. "He hadn't seen nothing, and he didn't know nothing. Then all of a sudden he started seeing things."

Nance said he'd told sheriff's investigators about his interview with McCraney, but they didn't seem to want to hear it.

Several days after the crime, Nance continued, Marvin Simpson had called from St. James Hospital, where he was recovering from injuries he'd just suffered in a car accident. Simpson said he knew who committed the crime, and it wasn't the men who'd been arrested.

Nance, who'd known Simpson since he was a child and trusted him, said he'd be right over. He asked if he could bring the sheriffs who were in charge of the investigation, and Simpson agreed.

When they arrived, Simpson named four men he believed killed Larry Lionberg and Carol Schmal.

Simpson's story made sense, Nance said, because two of the men he identified, Dennis and Ira Johnson, were "real trouble"—just the sort to have committed a rape and double murder. In contrast, Nance told Zorn, the men who'd been arrested and later convicted "never gave us any problems."

Asked if Simpson's lead had been pursued, Nance said Howard Vanick and David Capelli promised they'd follow up, but he doubted they ever did. "They were convinced the crime was already solved."

Zorn mentioned that he'd seen a street file summarizing the Simpson interview and asked if Nance had written it. Nance said he might have, since he'd taken notes, but he'd have to see it to know for sure. Zorn promised he'd get Nance a copy.

When the conversation ended, Zorn called Protess and recounted the interview. "Now I've got two columns," Zorn said, one on Gray for the next day's paper, one on Nance for two days later.

"I'll send the students down to show Nance the street file tomorrow," Protess said. "Maybe they can get more good stuff from him before your second column runs."

■ ■ ■

"Shaky to begin with, '78 murder case just got a lot flimsier," said the headline on Eric Zorn's February 13, 1996, column.

After summarizing his phone interview with Gray and the recantation she'd given to David Protess and the students, Zorn concluded: "Barring an un-recantation of Gray's un-recantation, the Jimerson case appears over, whether Jack O'Malley's office likes it or not. And this new development makes the other three convictions look dramatically weaker as well."

A copy of the column in hand, Protess went to channel 5 that morning, hoping to move producer Doug Longhini and reporter Tracy Haynes off the dime. They'd been preoccupied with February ratings sweeps pieces, and the Ford Heights Four story had slipped to the back burner.

But Longhini had been boning up on the case and had a surprise for Protess: He'd found 1978 file footage from the Homewood Clark station. The video showed, among other things, a distinctive leather vest like those reported stolen the night Larry Lionberg and Carol Schmal disappeared.

It was just what television needed—pictures.

Longhini wanted to show the video to René Brown, whose affidavit said Dennis Johnson had bought one of the stolen vests.

Protess, who hadn't located Brown, proposed having George Nance view the video, on the chance that he'd seen someone wearing such a vest after the crime. Perhaps Nance also would talk on camera about the street file, now that he'd spoken with Eric Zorn.

Grabbing the phone, Protess caught Laura Sullivan and Stephanie Goldstein on their way to show Nance the street file. He asked them to call him at channel 5 as soon as they arrived at Nance's home.

Protess then checked his voice mail, retrieving five messages from Paula Gray, each one increasingly hysterical. She'd been receiving anonymous, threatening calls in the wake of that morning's Eric Zorn column.

"We're gonna get you," she quoted one caller as saying.

"What do you want to do?" Protess asked, when he reached her.

"I don't know," she said. "I ain't got no place to go."

After conferring with Longhini, Protess extended an invitation: "How'd you like to stay in the Sheraton tonight? We'll get you a nice room right across from channel 5, and maybe you could do a short interview."

She agreed, and Protess said he'd have Laura and Stephanie pick her up and bring her downtown.

George Nance, as it turned out, hadn't been at home. And when the students called Protess, he told them there'd been a change in plans.

"Are you asking us to spend the night with Paula Gray?" Laura Sullivan wanted to know.

"It'll be like a slumber party." He laughed. "And you'll have the key to the honor bar."

As the students headed to Gray's apartment, Protess had one more call to make.

It was to an old friend, Thomas Decker, a lawyer who'd recently won freedom for a young Bible student, Steven Linscott, who'd been wrongly convicted of murder. Linscott had been exonerated by a new type of DNA test known as polymerase chain reaction (PCR), the same type of test the Ford Heights Four were now demanding. Decker had done Linscott's legal work *pro bono*, and Protess and Rob Warden had exposed the injustice.

Decker unhesitatingly agreed to represent Paula Gray.

After speaking with Gray, Decker put prosecutor Robert Milan on notice: No one from the state's attorney's office was to contact her again, in any manner, for any reason, without permission.

■ ■ ■

At a hastily arranged appearance before Judge Sheila Murphy the next day, February 14, Robert Milan announced that the state wanted DNA tests conducted after all.

Mark Ter Molen agreed on Verneal Jimerson's behalf.

Murphy, who'd long favored the testing, was delighted.

"Work out the details," she said. "I'm only concerned about one thing—that you get the best lab in the country."

She didn't ask what had prompted the state's change of heart, but she could guess.

She'd seen Eric Zorn's column, too.

■ ■ ■

On February 15, Eric Zorn struck again, this time with a column headlined, " 'Who' in whodunit might have been clear long ago."

The column disclosed the existence of the street file and quoted George Nance as saying the alternative suspects should have been pursued in 1978.

Tracy Haynes of channel 5 rushed to interview Nance, who relished appearing on camera.

When Haynes asked if he believed the Ford Heights Four were innocent, Nance cleaved the air with his hands, answering, "I believe it! I believe it! I don't care what nobody says, I believe it!"

Referring to the Marvin Simpson interview, Nance said the failure to pursue the other suspects had led to the convictions of the wrong men.

"I'm gonna be very frank, you understand me," Nance said. "I'd like to see the right [killers] caught.

"But they [the sheriff's investigators] buried the truth."

So taken was Haynes with the sound bites that he ended the interview without actually showing Nance the street file.

Despite the oversight, Doug Longhini produced a story titled "Falsely Accused?" that began with Haynes asking, "Were four men wrongly convicted because police withheld information and because their key witness lied?"

The story clearly suggested the answer with sound bites from George Nance and Paula Gray. (Said Gray: "The cops treated me like I was an animal, and I was afraid because there were six of them in the motel room with me.")

As the street file was shown on the screen, Haynes quoted from several excerpts and commented, "It raises questions about the integrity of the investigation and trial."

■ ■ ■

"We're ready to do a ton of stories on this case," Doug Longhini told David Protess after the broadcast.

"Get a good reaction from the news director?" Protess asked.

"No, he doesn't give a shit, but Tracy Haynes and I do," Longhini replied. "What else you got?"

"René Brown. I found him, and he'll talk to us."

■ ■ ■

René Brown had given up criminal investigations and was running a small grocery store in a high-crime area on Chicago's south side.

At midday, when Doug Longhini and David Protess arrived with a camera crew, Brown had not yet opened for business. The windows were shuttered with burglar bars, the sidewalk littered with fast-food wrappers and broken beer bottles.

Brown unlocked the door and introduced himself, firmly shaking hands. He wore a black sweater and a tattered baseball cap. A cigarette dangled from his mouth, and there was a faint odor of liquor on his breath.

While the crew set up in one of the narrow aisles, Longhini explained that he first wanted Brown's recollections of his interviews with Dennis Johnson. "Then I'll show you some documents," Longhini said.

The camera rolling, Brown said Johnson had mentioned the .38, the deuce and a quarter, and items taken from the Clark station, "including some leather vests."

"Did he say where the vests were made?" Longhini asked.

"The leather was from Mexico," said Brown.

Longhini showed Brown a 1978 crime-scene report saying the vests bore a label, *Hecho en Mexico*.

"The cops knew that back then?" Brown said with surprise.

"Not only that," said Longhini, reaching for the street file. "Take a look at this."

As Brown read, he shook his head and thumped the document with his fingers.

"This report reflects what I found out years later," he said. "It means they knew. They knew all along."

Tears filled his eyes.

"What do you think should be done?" Longhini asked.

"The cops should reopen the investigation," Brown replied. "Families on both sides deserve justice. We all deserve justice."

After the interview, Brown took Protess aside.

"I gotta get back into this case," he said. "I'll do whatever you need."

Protess hesitated.

"Please," Brown implored. "It'll be my salvation."

12

Voices from the Grave

■ René Brown's plea could not be denied.

Fate intervened when a relative of Willie Rainge ran into Dennis and Ira Johnson's father, Sam, in Ford Heights, got his address, and passed it along to David Protess.

It seemed an ideal opportunity to bring Brown back into the case: Since Brown had known Dennis Johnson, his presence might break the ice with the elder Johnson.

Brown was ready to go when Protess picked him up on a windy March morning a few days after Brown's interview aired on channel 5.

"Like the channel 5 piece?" Protess asked on the way to Ford Heights.

"Wasn't bad."

"First time you were ever on TV?"

Brown fell silent.

"Well?" Protess prodded.

Groping for words, Brown finally said, "There was another time."

He remembered the exact date: December 17, 1990. It was the day after his father had been murdered.

Three neighborhood youths had robbed the grocery store, the one Brown now ran, and shot Nathaniel Brown in the heart. He was seventy-one years old.

"My dad was a public school teacher for twenty years," Brown said. "The store was his retirement. Everyone liked him. And for me, he was my only hero."

Applying the skills he'd honed as a defense investigator, Brown helped police track down the killers, two aged fourteen, one fifteen. They were convicted of murder.

It was Brown's last case—until today.

■ ■ ■

An old man with a cane hobbled along the street in front of a row of brick tenements on the edge of Ford Heights.

"I betcha that's him," said David Protess, bolting from the car.

"Sam?" said Protess, extending his hand.

Sam Johnson nodded and accepted the handshake.

"I'm Dave Protess, and this is René Brown. He knew your son Dennis."

Johnson invited them into his apartment and introduced them to his girlfriend, a fiftyish woman named Barbara, who served him a plate of bacon and eggs.

Seated in the tiny living room, straining to be heard over the blare of a television set, Brown began, "Your son was a man. He wanted to stand up and tell the truth about those two white people killed in the projects. He knew the wrong men were in jail, and he wanted to help them."

Placing a tape recorder on a coffee table, Protess interjected, "Did your son ever tell you about it?"

"Dennis and Ira, they told me what happened," he said in a raspy voice. "They said they took the woman to the apartment and misused her."

"What'd *you* say then?" Brown asked.

"I told them they should give themselves up."

Johnson added that Dennis and Ira then "went to Detroit and laid low for a while." After they came home, "it wasn't spoke of no more."

Protess asked if they'd ever mentioned the type of gun used in the crime.

Johnson's brow furrowed. "My boys didn't hurt nobody," he suddenly declared.

"But I've got what you just said on tape," Protess said. "Barbara, you heard him say they 'misused' the woman, didn't you?"

"You said that, Sam," Barbara confirmed.

"My brain's fried," he said. "I had a stroke, an' I don't remember nothin' too well."

With that, he announced that he was late for a poker game and had to leave.

At Brown's insistence, Johnson accepted a ride.

The poker game, it turned out, was in the Ford Heights municipal building, which housed the police station.

When Brown expressed amusement, Johnson said, "It's all right. I've knowed the chief more than twenty years."

"We've heard you're a powerful man in town," Brown fished.

"Well," Johnson beamed as he got out of the car, "I got the mayor elected—four times."

■ ■ ■

The next day, David Protess, Stephanie Goldstein, and Stacey Delo went to see Willie Rainge at the Pontiac Correctional Center, where he'd just been transferred from Stateville.

The primary purpose of the visit was to find out what, if anything, Rainge knew about the suspects identified in the street file. Protess hadn't wanted to discuss that on the phone because prison calls were monitored.

After greeting Protess with a long embrace, Rainge bowed politely and shook hands with the students. He had a braided ponytail, now with conspicuous strands of gray, and wore brown tortoiseshell glasses.

Rainge said he'd heard about the interview that spawned the street file from his most recent appellate attorney, with whom he lost contact when she went on maternity leave.

He wasn't at all surprised that the Johnson brothers had been identified as suspects. Dennis Johnson, he said, "was a mean m-f, know what I'm sayin'?" and Ira "was fond of throwin' rocks at kids in the neighborhood."

Protess described the Sam Johnson interview, and Rainge said he'd seen the old man driving around the Heights in the seventies in a "ragtop deuce and a quarter." Maybe that was the car used in the crime, speculated Rainge, who'd never heard of Johnny Rodriguez.

Rainge didn't know Red Robinson either, but did have a lead on where he might be. Red's younger brother, Curt Robinson, had fathered two children by Patricia Hatten, Rainge's former girlfriend. Hatten also was the mother of Rainge's daughter, Arealya, who'd mentioned in passing that Curt and Red were living together in Ford Heights. Although Rainge didn't know precisely where, he thought Hatten might know, and he provided her address and phone number.

When Delo asked about how Rainge's children were doing, he said Arealya, now twenty-one, had recently had a baby, making him a grandfather. She'd been living in Minnesota, but had moved back to live with Hatten and applied to join the Job Corps.

Rainge's son, Tederol, now nineteen, was in special public housing for the handicapped. Two years earlier, Tederol had been robbed and shot, leaving him paralyzed from the waist down.

"When they arrested me, Tederol wasn't old enough to walk, and now I don't know if I'll ever see him walk," Rainge said. "If I could've been a father to him, it wouldn't have happened."

When the interview time drew to a close, Rainge called Protess aside and confided something he hadn't wanted to say "in front of the girls."

He was afraid.

His transfer to gang-controlled Pontiac occurred "as soon as the media started tellin' the truth about us." He no longer was "hooked up" with the Black Disciples and had put in a request for protective custody, but it had been denied.

"I may not live to see justice," he said.

Protess said he'd try to get him legal help, and left the prison contemplating which lawyer's arm he was going to have to twist next.

■ ■ ■

On the way home, David Protess and the students stopped in rural St. Anne, hoping to interview Charles McCraney. He wasn't in, so Protess left his phone number with a haggard-looking neighbor, whom Stacey Delo thought resembled one of the killers in the movie *Deliverance*.

That evening, relaxing in his living room chair, Protess dozed off and dreamed that Willie Rainge had been murdered with a crossbow—a sure sign, Protess thought, that Rainge needed a lawyer right away.

Protess called a colleague, Northwestern University Law School Professor Lawrence Marshall. Five months earlier, a team of lawyers led by Marshall had won a long fight on behalf of Rolando Cruz, an innocent man who'd twice been sentenced to die for the murder of a ten-year-old girl in suburban DuPage County.

Chicago Lawyer had exposed the injustice in a series of articles beginning in 1983, and Eric Zorn had taken up the cause in more than fifty *Tribune* columns. The reporting left little doubt that the murder had been committed by a confessed killer named Brian Dugan.

Finally, Cruz and a codefendant, Alex Hernandez, were exonerated by PCR-type DNA testing, which linked Dugan to the crime. Police and prosecutors were now facing criminal charges for allegedly fabricating evidence against Cruz and Hernandez.

After listening patiently to Protess, Marshall agreed to try to get Rainge moved to a safer environment and to assign a couple of law students to the case. Marshall said he wouldn't be able to handle Rainge's case alone, but might enlist the help of one of his cocounsels in the Cruz case, Matthew Kennelly, an expert on DNA.

"I've been leaning on Matt to represent Dennis Williams," said Protess. (On February 20, Williams had fired his lawyer for "inexcusable unresponsiveness" to his letters and phone calls.)

"Why don't you see if Bob Byman will take Dennis?" Marshall suggested.

■ ■ ■

David Protess had been reluctant to ask any more favors of Jenner & Block partner Robert Byman. At the instigation of Protess and Rob Warden, Byman had devoted eight hundred hours of *pro bono* time to exonerating David Dowaliby, the working-class suburban man whose daughter had been abducted from the family home and murdered.

At Dennis Williams's prodding, however, Protess approached Byman, with considerable trepidation.

Indeed, Byman was hesitant to get involved, although not for the reason Protess had anticipated.

While Byman was more than willing to volunteer his time, he was concerned about the prospect of losing a capital case. He'd seen firsthand the emotional toll the Girvies Davis and Hernando Williams cases had exacted from other Jenner & Block lawyers in the past year.

"But we're gonna win this one," said Protess, showing Byman the street file and describing the Sam Johnson interview.

"Tell you what, Dave," Byman finally said, half jokingly, "I'll take the case on one condition—that you promise to solve the crime."

■ ■ ■

The pressure was on.

The Illinois Supreme Court was on the verge of setting an execution date for Dennis Williams. And Robert Byman thought the only way to stop that would be to come up with solid evidence of Williams's innocence.

To that end, David Protess again turned to René Brown.

The first order of business was to see Willie Rainge's former girlfriend, Patricia Hatten.

When Brown called to arrange a meeting, he told her about the 1978 police interview with Marvin Simpson and asked if Red and Curt Robinson still lived in the Heights.

Not only did they, she replied, but so did Marvin Simpson.

"Marvin's dead," said Brown.

"No he's not," said Hatten. "I just saw him."

Simpson was her neighbor, as were the Robinsons.

■ ■ ■

René Brown and David Protess got there as fast as they could.

They were welcomed by Patricia Hatten and her daughter by Willie Rainge, Arealya.

Protess filled them in on his recent visit with Rainge and the latest developments in the case. Showing them the street file, he said he wondered if the Marvin Simpson they knew could be the man quoted in the report.

"I'll try to get him on the phone," Arealya offered.

She made the call from her mother's bedroom and emerged a few moments later, asking, "Which one of you wants to talk to him?"

"He's all yours, René," said Protess.

"Marvin," Brown began, "were you ever married to a Loretta Simpson?"

"Never been married."

"Know anyone else named Marvin Simpson?"

"Jus' me. Why?"

"Marvin, you're not dead!"

"Still tickin', praise the Lord."

"Were you in St. James Hospital back in '78?"

"Uh, yeah."

"And you told some cops about a crime you knew about?"

"Oh, man, I've had a lot of hurtin' over that."

"Will you talk to my friend and me about it?"

"Not now."

"Some innocent lives are at stake here, and you may be able to help."

"I'll think on it."

"Will you, man?"

"I promise."

Brown gave him his phone number, asking Simpson to call.

A beaming Brown returned to the living room, declaring, "He's the guy. He had to be alive—he was too important to be dead."

"That's incredible," Protess responded, marveling at the coincidence: two Marvin Simpsons, both African-Americans, both with connections to the Heights, both born the same year.

While Brown recounted the phone conversation, a nervous-looking woman arrived. Hatten introduced her as Marian Walk.

"You ain't no cops, are ya?" she asked.

After Protess showed her his Northwestern faculty ID, she revealed she was the sister of David Jackson, the jailhouse snitch.

Her brother, she said, "felt guilty for what he done" and had recanted "to make it right."

"We'd like to talk to him," said Protess.

"You can't," she said. "He died from AIDS."

But he'd told her something important before his death—that he'd been put up to snitching by Bernard Robinson, another of Red's brothers.

Four days after the murders, Bernard and David Jackson were arrested for burglary and wound up in the county jail with Dennis Williams and Willie Rainge.

Bernard had encouraged him to implicate Williams and Rainge, Jackson had claimed, to draw suspicion away from Red. And the prosecutors had been happy to drop the charge against Jackson, as long as he stuck to his story, which they helped him concoct.

"Jesus," Brown muttered. "Can you show us where the Robinsons live?"

Bernard had moved away, but Red and Curt lived down the block with their mother, Dorothy. Going to the front window and pointing to a house, Walk said, "That's where they lives."

"And where do you live?" Protess asked.

She then pointed to a house Protess recognized. He'd been there with the students. It was the crack house.

■ ■ ■

Ira Johnson turned out to be a disappointment.

After finally agreeing to see Laura Sullivan and Stacey Delo, he professed no knowledge of the crime. He mostly just leered at the visitors, particularly Delo.

Johnson also declared himself innocent of murdering Cherry Wilder, claiming his confession had been coerced.

As they prepared to leave, Sullivan showed him the street file, pointing out the passage saying he'd panicked when Larry Lionberg's body was discovered.

"That's bull jive," he said. "I jus' didn't want to see no dead body."

"What about your .38?" she asked.

"There was a lot of guns floatin' around back then." He paused, smiling. "What *did* I do with that .38?"

He would say no more.

■ ■ ■

On the same trip to Menard, the students visited Dennis Williams in the Condemned Unit.

The only name Williams recognized in the street file was Ira Johnson's.

Williams remembered him well.

As a teenager, Williams had been the target of one of Johnson's rock-throwing sprees, to which Williams had responded by rendering his tormenter unconscious with a two-by-four.

When Sam Johnson came over to complain to Williams's mother, Lula, she kicked him out of her house.

After that, Ira and Dennis kept their distance, as did Sam and Lula.

■ ■ ■

Marvin Simpson never called, so David Protess and René Brown decided to plead their case in person.

When they appeared on his front porch, he opened the door, holding a plate of greasy scrambled eggs. Guessing who they were, he said, "I'm gonna talk to you. I decided."

"How'd you like to go to a nice restaurant?" Protess asked.

"Ain't no restaurants in Ford Heights, but there's a good chicken place in Chicago Heights," he said agreeably.

"Let's go," said Protess.

The chicken place was a fast-food, take-out joint, but Brown spotted a comfortable-looking restaurant next door, Biamonte's Family Dining, which Simpson was game for trying. The three slid into a secluded booth.

Simpson, forty-one years old, was an affable, round-faced, dark-skinned man with graying, braided hair, sparkling white teeth, and a gold wire earring in his left earlobe. He went by the nickname Moon, acquired because "my daddy used to shave my head when I was a little kid, an' it shined like th' moon."

He said he'd been hesitant to talk for several reasons: No one had paid attention to what he'd said initially, he feared the Johnsons, and one man involved in the crime "is like a brother to me."

Brown assured him that he and Protess were thoroughly investigating the case and, as for the Johnsons, Dennis was dead and Ira was in prison.

But, Simpson said, several members of the family remained in Ford Heights and had "connections."

"Sam Johnson's already told us his sons confessed the crime to him," said Protess.

"You can just tell us the story without naming the friend you want to protect," Brown suggested.

"I'll tell ya what I can," Simpson offered.

■ ■ ■

On May 10, 1978, Marvin and nine or ten other young men were sitting under a huge oak tree at the west edge of the projects, drinking beer and smoking marijuana.

"Dennis Johnson popped up outta nowhere and offered ten dollars to anybody who'd take him somewhere to pick up some money. He didn't say where. I probably woulda taken him, 'cept my car wasn't runnin.' If my radiator hadn't been busted, I'd a gone for that ten dollars.

"That's when Johnny [Rodriguez] said he'd drive him. Johnny was drunk on that Budweiser and he said, 'Hell, yes, I'll take you.' Dennis and Johnny climbed into Johnny's deuce and a quarter, an' they peeled out. I knew Dennis wasn't up to no good, 'cause I knew the Dude."

Later that night, Marvin continued, he went to see Connie Moses, a girlfriend who lived a few houses down from Paula Gray, across the courtyard from the abandoned townhouse.

"I jus' got hot and horny, an' I went over there to get with Connie. Connie was in th' house, and I was sittin' on th' porch, jus' waitin' in th' dark. I heard a couple of shots. I thought maybe they was firecrackers. Five minutes or so later there was a couple more.

"Then I seen Ira come runnin' through th' gangway. He stopped real quick, like he was lookin' for somebody. I jus' thought maybe he'd stole a car radio or somethin'."

Marvin said he could see Ira because he was illuminated by a streetlight on Cannon Lane, but Ira couldn't see Marvin because it was dark where he was sitting. "If he'd've seen me I probably wouldn't be here now. He'd've killed me sure.

"Come mornin' they was sellin' cigarettes outta th' trunk of th' deuce and a quarter. Dennis was wearin' a buckskin vest he didn't have when I seen 'im the night before. I asked, 'How much you sellin' them cigarettes for?' Maybe it was fifty cents a pack. I got me three packs."

A day later, May 12, Marvin said he was working on his car in the gangway adjacent to the building in the projects where he lived. Ira was watching him.

"Kids come runnin' across th' street, sayin', 'They found some bodies! They found some bodies!' I headed over there. I looked back an' said, 'Hey, Ira, ain't you comin'?' He got real nervous an' said, 'I don't want to see no bodies.' "

That night, Ira's younger brother, Tannie, told Marvin that Ira was trying to sell a .38. When Marvin asked Ira about the gun, he said he'd already sold it to a man named Melvin Strayhorn, during a crap game.

On May 13, Marvin was driving home from a club, thinking about whether he should go to the police, when his car was rear-ended. He wound up in St. James Hospital with a broken back.

"In th' hospital, I was lookin' at th' news. Four guys got arrested. I thought, 'No, they got th' wrong people.' I got to churnin' inside, wonderin' whether I should tell anybody about it or not.

"Finally, I decides to call George Nance cause he was th' only one I could trust up there. I called a few times an' told the dispatcher lady that I had to see Lieutenant Nance about them murders. But I didn't hear nothin' back for a couple a days.

"When George finally shows up, there's two white cops with him. They was up there an hour or two. George an' one of th' white officers was writin' things down, but I never heard from 'em after that.

"When I run into George on the street after I got outta th' hospital, he said them white cops jus' didn't wanta listen."

■ ■ ■

"Did you tell the cops everything you just told us?" René Brown asked.

"Yup, sure did," said Marvin Simpson.

"Take a look at this," said Brown, handing him the street file.

"Can't read."

Brown read parts of the narrative aloud, drawing Simpson's attention to the most notable omission: There was nothing in the report about Simpson hearing shots and seeing Ira Johnson run away from the abandoned townhouse.

"I told 'em that. You can ask George."

When Brown pointed out that the report didn't mention Dennis Johnson wearing a buckskin vest after the crime, Simpson responded, "They was all wearin' 'em."

"All?" Protess asked. "Dennis, Ira, Johnny—who else?"

Simpson grimaced.

"Moon, you *told* the cops about Red Robinson," Protess said. "It's right here in the report."

Simpson nodded. "George asked me to tell 'em the truth, an' I did."

"Was Red wearing a vest, too?" Protess asked.

Simpson again nodded. "He might even still have it," he said, explaining that Robinson had worn the vest for years and wasn't the type to throw out anything.

"We'd buy that vest from him," said Protess. "Can you talk to him about it?"

"I'll think on it," Simpson said. "I ain't sure what's right anymore."

He'd tried to do the right thing in 1978, Simpson explained, but nothing happened. Then, when Ira Johnson killed Cherry Wilder in 1991, "it started hurtin' all over again." Feeling responsible for the murder, Simpson developed a bleeding ulcer.

After that, with Ira in prison and Dennis dead, Simpson had tried to put the crime out of his mind. He'd hoped the day would never come when he'd again have to implicate Red Robinson, a lifelong friend.

"What about the guys in prison doin' his time?" Brown asked.

"That's why I decided to talk to y'all. That's why I'll try to do what I can."

■ ■ ■

The bald, stocky retired cop put on his reading glasses and studied the street file, reading it twice, muttering from time to time, before sharing his thoughts.

"This ain't my report," George Nance finally said, "and it ain't all here."

"Well, whose is it?" asked René Brown.

"It has to be that young cop's—Capelli," Nance said. "I think his first name's Dave."

"What'd you mean, it isn't all here?" David Protess asked.

"I mean it's sanitized. It don't have some of the best things Marvin Simpson told us."

Nance described Simpson as "an eyewitness to the crime," adding, "He saw two of the killers flee the scene."

"Two?" Brown asked. "Which two?"

Looking at the street file, Nance answered, "Red Robinson and Ira Johnson. Marvin heard four or five gunshots, and then he saw Red come runnin' around the side of the townhouse. Ira was followin' with a gun in his hand."

Brown and Protess glanced at each other, realizing Simpson had held back the crucial detail that he'd seen Red at the murder scene.

"Was Red the kind of kid who'd commit a crime like this?" Protess asked.

"I wouldn't have thought so, but he could've fallen in with the wrong crowd, and the Johnsons were the wrong crowd for sure."

Dennis and Ira thought they could get away with anything because "their folks had clout," Nance continued. Sam and Marcella Johnson sponsored political rallies for Mayor Saul Beck, and on election day they turned out the vote.

And Beck rewarded Marcella by naming her, "this mother of two gangsters," to the police board. The position gave her power over police personnel, including Police Chief Jack Davis, and access to investigative information.

"Would she have seen your notes on the Simpson interview?" Brown asked.

"I had to turn them over to Jack Davis, which was the same as turnin' them over to Marcella Johnson."

Nance's notes had never surfaced, and he assumed they'd been destroyed.

But even more troubling, Nance said, was that he hadn't received Marvin Simpson's phone messages for two days. In the interim, Paula Gray had testified before the grand jury, and the authorities had announced that they'd caught the killers.

"For whatever reason, the dispatcher didn't tell me about Marvin's calls," Nance said. "If we'd interviewed him when he first called, the sheriffs might've checked out what he said and this whole thing could've turned out different."

"But George," Protess said, saving the most touchy question for last, "why didn't you come forward with this before?"

"Chief Davis and the sheriffs ordered me not to," Nance replied with bitterness. "What was I supposed to do?"

Then he sighed.

"I guess I was just too weak to stand up to them, and finally I quit the force. But I always swore I'd tell the truth if anybody asked me."

13

Advantageous Attraction

■ Mail spilled onto Medill's mauve carpet as David Protess cleared out his overflowing faculty box on March 13, 1996, the first day he'd been on campus in a week.

Picking up the pile, he spotted a white envelope addressed, in his care, to Stacey. It was from Ira Johnson, who'd scrawled "SWAK"—sealed with a kiss—on the back.

Protess tore open the letter.

"Hello Beautiful," it began. After wishing her well, Johnson got to the point: "I really had a nice time with you and Laura and I *did* have things to talk about, but I'm not going to get myself in that shit."

However, a few lines later, he seemed to have a change of heart: "Maybe you *will* get the opportunity to hear what you been wanting to hear."

Johnson explained why: "I couldn't get you off my mind, all I could think about was your bedroom eyes—they are very, very, very, sexy looking. . . . Stacey, you are one sexy-ass woman to be a white girl." If she returned for another visit, he promised, "it well may be worth your time."

But he placed several conditions on another interview: It had to take place in the regular visiting area of the prison (rather than the interview room), she had to pose for a picture with him, and Laura couldn't be present.

"We can drink a soda and eat a little popcorn like getting to know one another," he wrote. "I wish I could have met you years ago. I bet you would have been my woman."

The seven-page, handwritten letter closed, "Your new friend, Ira." There was a postscript: "I didn't get your last name so you are going to be Stacey Johnson for now. Okay?"

Rummaging through the mail, Protess found another white envelope, this one addressed to Laura. The letter was less than half the length of Stacey's and a bit more businesslike.

Laura Sullivan had aggressively questioned Johnson during the interview, and now Johnson posed one in return: "Did it seem to you that I was lying?" he asked.

"I want you to answer that whenever we meet again. I'm hoping it [will] be soon, because I would love to see that fat ass of yours.

"Laura," he continued, "think about getting what you been trying to find out—you know them boys didn't do that shit and I know this also."

Inviting her to return to Menard to learn the truth, he backed off one of the conditions he'd imposed in the letter to Stacey. He'd see them together—as long as it was in the visiting area.

"We might be able to accomplish something," he wrote.

"Love you for a friend, I. B. J."

■ ■ ■

Sitting side by side in David Protess's office that afternoon, Stacey Delo and Laura Sullivan scoured the letters.

Stephanie Goldstein peered over their shoulders as they gasped and tittered.

Delo, blushing, finally put down her letter.

Sullivan declared, "I'm going down there and kick his ass."

"No one's going anywhere until we've thought this through," Protess said.

Johnson clearly was offering to talk about the crime, Protess mused, but how much would he say? While Johnson was already serving a long prison term, admitting to murdering Larry Lionberg and Carol Schmal would make him eligible for the death penalty.

Then there were the obvious safety issues, which argued against Delo and Sullivan seeing Johnson in the largely unsupervised visiting area unless Protess went along. And they'd be allowed to tape-record the interview only if it were done in a conference room reserved for lawyers and journalists.

"How would you feel about having your picture taken with Ira?" he asked.

Sullivan didn't seem to mind, as long as Johnson didn't touch her. Delo, still not recovered from reading her letter, didn't like the idea at all, but was willing to be present for the interview.

"I'll go, too," Goldstein volunteered. As the others looked at her with surprise, she added, "I want to be there for you if you decide to do this."

Protess said he was proud of her, and had little doubt that Johnson wouldn't object to having a third female visitor. But they should discuss it with their families and friends, and Protess needed to talk it over with the dean.

Meanwhile, they agreed there would be no harm in Delo and Sullivan answering the letters, letting Johnson know they would consider returning only if he had something genuinely significant to say.

"Tell him to write you back with a hint of what he's willing to talk about," Protess said. "He'll probably do that—he's obviously desperate for company."

"Thanks a lot," Delo said.

■ ■ ■

On March 15, Charles McCraney's appearance was anxiously awaited at a Kentucky Fried Chicken in Kankakee, Illinois.

Paul Ciolino's hair was slicked back. The private investigator wore a sharkskin suit and white-on-white shirt with gold cuff links, his tie secured by an ornate pin.

Sitting opposite him were David Protess and René Brown, dressed down for the occasion.

McCraney, after receiving Protess's hand-delivered note, had called and promised to be there, but he already was two hours late.

The trio was about to give up when in he walked.

Protess introduced himself and then Brown. "And this is Jerry Bruckheimer, the Hollywood producer I was telling you about," said Protess as Ciolino extended his hand.

"Please have a seat, Charlie," said Ciolino.

McCraney did as he was told.

"Here's the deal, Charlie," Ciolino said. "If you're willing to tell your story, it could be worth something."

"How 'bout startin' by payin' for my time?" said McCraney, claiming he'd interrupted his workday to be there.

Ciolino pulled out a gold money clip, peeled off four crisp twenties, and tossed them on the table.

"Whatcha wanna know?" McCraney inquired, pocketing the cash.

"Just the truth about what you saw back in nineteen seventy-eight," Ciolino replied.

McCraney leaped to his feet. "I ain't talkin' 'bout that no more," he declared.

"Isn't my money as good as the prosecutors'?" Ciolino asked. "They paid you, didn't they?"

"Not as much as you might think," McCraney said. Then he paused, stroking his chin.

"Let me get back to you," he finally said.

"You know how to reach me," Protess said as McCraney left the restaurant.

■ ■ ■

When he got home a couple of hours later, David Protess checked his office voice mail.

There was one message—from Charles McCraney.

"If you pay me up front," it said, "I'll tell you whatever you wanna hear."

Protess called him back and said, "Charlie, your story may be worth something someday, but only if you tell us the truth first."

"Money up front, or no talk," McCraney snapped. "That's that."

"As I suspected, Charlie," Protess told him, "you're nothing but a whore."

■ ■ ■

Charles McCraney summoned state's attorney's investigators to complain about David Protess, René Brown, and the man he knew as Jerry Bruckheimer.

According to the investigators' report, McCraney claimed they'd "offered him $250,000 with 20 percent up front for him to come on their side.

"The money was to be delivered to McCraney's house by a woman . . . and if he wanted to use the woman for a couple of days, he could."

When the investigators asked McCraney to recall the events of May 10–11, 1978, he was "adamant" that he'd heard the gunshot from the direction of the abandoned townhouse at "approximately 12:30 A.M."

Since "the actual occurrence could not have occurred before 2:30 A.M.," said the report, "it is surely reasonable to assume that he is mistaken."

■ ■ ■

As spring approached, Willie Rainge's new lawyer, Professor Lawrence Marshall, convened a strategy session over brunch at the Orrington Hotel in Evanston.

Present were Rob Warden, David Protess, Stephanie Goldstein, and Matthew Kennelly, who'd signed on as Marshall's cocounsel.

Before getting down to business, the guests toasted Marshall for recent back-to-back legal victories.

Based on a strong factual claim of innocence, he'd won a new trial for a young vegetable farmer, Gary Gauger, who'd been sentenced to death for murdering his parents. And he and Robert Byman had persuaded Judge Frank Meekins to drop his opposition to DNA testing in the Willie Rainge and Dennis Williams cases, giving Sheila Murphy control of the arrangements.

After obligatory sips of champagne, the lawyers outlined three legal hurdles that lay ahead for the Ford Heights Four.

First, Kenny Adams, unlike the others, had exhausted his appellate remedies. Marshall feared that under new habeas corpus legislation pending in Congress and supported by the White House, Adams might forever be barred from raising his claim of innocence. He needed a lawyer immediately.

"I'm out of lawyers," Protess groaned. But Marshall had already talked to one, Jeffrey Urdangen, who'd successfully represented Rolando Cruz's codefendant, Alex Hernandez. "Jeff's waiting for your call," said Marshall.

Next, the DNA testing could be delayed indefinitely unless both sides agreed on an expert. Kennelly wanted Dr. Edward Blake to do the tests, but the prosecutors wanted Cellmark Diagnostics in Germantown, Maryland.

Now it was Warden's turn to groan. The director of operations at Cellmark was Mark Stolorow, who'd previously been the chief serologist at the Illinois State Police Crime Lab. "He was a shameless apologist for the state's mistakes in two cases we exposed in *Chicago Lawyer*," said Warden.

"Well, there's no way the prosecutors are going to accept Blake," said Kennelly.

"How about Bing?" Warden suggested.

Dr. David Bing, a Harvard Medical School professor who headed CBR Laboratories in Boston, was respected by both prosecutors and defense lawyers. At the state's request, he'd conducted the tests that exonerated Steven Linscott, the Bible student who'd been represented by Thomas Decker, now Paula Gray's lawyer.

Kennelly, a Harvard man himself, thought Bing would be a terrific compromise. He ran one of the few labs in the country capable of PCR-type DNA testing. "If anyone besides Ed Blake can find semen on what's left of that vaginal swab," Kennelly said, "it's Dave Bing."

As long as Robert Byman and Mark Ter Molen agreed, Kennelly would propose Bing to the prosecutors before Judge Murphy took up the issue a few days hence.

Finally, to build the case for innocence, Marshall wanted to memorialize the interviews concerning the alternative suspects. "We'll need affidavits from people like George Nance and Marvin Simpson," he said.

"I've already talked to René Brown about that," Protess said, "and Stephanie here has agreed to help."

"It'll be a valuable experience," Marshall told Goldstein, who was planning to go to law school in the fall.

"And if you can get a good affidavit from your new pen pal," he added, referring to Ira Johnson, "we may not have to worry about anything else."

■ ■ ■

Fearful that an impasse over a DNA expert could prompt Judge Murphy to appoint Dr. Edward Blake, the prosecutors agreed on March 20 to accept Matthew Kennelly's compromise candidate.

With the stroke of a pen the next day, Murphy approved the appointment of Dr. David Bing to do the tests.

The state's attorney's office would arrange to send Bing the vaginal swab and a laboratory slide that had been used in the original serological testing.

The defense lawyers would arrange for their clients to provide fresh blood and saliva samples from which Bing could extract DNA to compare with any genetic material he might detect on the swab or slide.

The lawyers told Murphy they'd report back with the results of the tests in about a month.

Outside the courtroom, Marshall, whom the defense lawyers had elected as spokesperson, did an on-camera interview with channel 5's Tracy Haynes.

"The defendants have been waiting for this moment for years," said Marshall. "They are very hopeful that these tests will prove what they have said all along, which is that they are innocent men."

Privately, however, Marshall was worried.

David Bing and Edward Blake had used the same word to describe the chance of finding DNA on the eighteen-year-old swab and slide: "Remote."

And the authorities had rejected Marshall's pleas to put Willie Rainge into protective custody at Pontiac, leaving him in mortal danger.

■ ■ ■

Ira Johnson wrote to Stacey and Laura in care of David Protess on March 31:

I don't want to see them guys die for some shit they didn't do. I know all about that murder. I know who shot the girl and her boyfriend.

I can't live with this shit anymore. I can't let this shit keep haunting me. I haven't been able to sleep, thinking about if they kill them boys, I couldn't live with it.

So if you like to hear what went on that night when them two people got killed, just take that trip down here.

I'm going to let you know a little something, okay? They rode around for about an hour and then they hesitated and went to that apartment, and that's where it all ended.

It's a long story. With the shit I know, them brothers shouldn't have any problems getting a new trial.

Maybe God will bless me for saving them boys' life. Them boys done suffered damn near twenty years for some shit they know nothing about.

Come down, and you won't be wasting your time.

■ ■ ■

Although the winter school term had ended—and the students had aced Protess's investigative reporting class—they weren't about to stop now.

They signed on to continue investigating the case as an independent study project in the final term of their senior year.

Their first assignment: Get a confession from Ira Johnson.

In his letters, Johnson had dropped his insistence on seeing the students in the visiting area of the prison.

He still wanted to have pictures taken, however. Stacey Delo reluctantly agreed to pose for the cause, and Stephanie Goldstein volunteered to be the photographer.

David Protess would go along for safety's sake—that would appease the dean—and to draft an affidavit for Johnson to sign if he confessed.

Goldstein handled the arrangements, securing permission from the Illinois Department of Corrections to take a tape recorder and Polaroid camera into the prison for an interview with Ira Johnson in April, as soon as the students returned from spring break.

■ ■ ■

The Chicago Bulls were playing a nationally televised game on Sunday, March 24, so David Protess and René Brown thought they'd find the men they were looking for at home.

Marvin Simpson, who fortunately wasn't a Bulls fan, agreed to serve as their guide. Through a little detective work of his own, he'd located Johnny Rodriguez living near the Ford Heights municipal building, a short walk from the old oak tree where Simpson said the crime had been planned.

While Protess and Brown waited in the car, Simpson knocked on the door and was greeted by a mustached man in a white T-shirt. Simpson emerged moments later only to report, "He won't talk to ya."

"Don't blame him," Brown said.

The next stop was on the south end of Ford Heights, the apartment of David Campbell, one of the men Simpson said had been present for the colloquy that preceded the crime. Campbell *was* a Bulls fan and didn't want to be interrupted. But he made an offer that couldn't be refused: He'd meet them after the game at Red Robinson's house.

Campbell's promise to join them made Simpson feel more comfortable about involving the friend he'd wanted to protect. What happened next was up to Red.

Protess, Brown, and Simpson drove around for the next hour or so, picking up a bucket of KFC and listening to the game on the radio. They pulled up in front of Red's place just as Michael Jordan missed a last-second layup and the Bulls lost by a point to the lowly Toronto Raptors.

A chorus of howls echoed from the household.

"Maybe we should come back," Protess suggested, but Simpson was already halfway up the walk.

"If he lets us in, should I bring my piece?" Brown asked Protess.

"No, it sounds like we're outnumbered," said Protess. "A Bible might be better."

Simpson was back in a flash. "Red'll see ya."

Replays of M. J.'s miss on a forty-eight-inch color screen dominated the attention of the assemblage, which included Red and Curt Robinson, their mother Dorothy, and assorted relatives.

Brown plopped down next to Red on the living room couch, and Protess took a chair to Red's right, while Marvin went into the kitchen with Curt.

After commiserating over the Bulls' loss, Brown told Robinson, "You know why we're here."

Red nodded.

"Did the cops ever interview you about the crime?" Brown asked.

"No."

"What can you tell us about it?" Protess asked.

"Don't know much," said Robinson, who was a dead ringer for Yankee outfielder Darryl Strawberry. "I was there that night when they was sellin' stuff from the car. I bought one of them buckskin vests."

"Who'd you buy it from?"

"Dennis Johnson. Ira was there, too."

"How much?"

"Ten dollars."

"You still have it?"

"Could be in the basement. I'll look later."

Not wanting to push him further, Protess asked him to repeat what he'd just said on tape, and he agreed.

As he was doing that, a bearded mountain of a man entered without a knock and took a chair across from Brown.

David Campbell's booming voice commanded the attention of all present, including Dorothy Robinson, who turned her head from the tube for the first time.

"The man that did that crime was Dennis Johnson, him an' his little brother Ira," said Campbell.

Campbell corroborated Simpson's account of events before the crime, conspicuously omitting Red and Johnny Rodriguez, but adding that Dennis and Ira had been shooting heroin that day.

"Dennis was a stone-cold killer," said Campbell. "I seen him once almost strangle a girl to death. If I hadn't been there to pull him off, there'd a been another murder."

Asked about the buckskin vests, Campbell said he'd seen Dennis Johnson wearing one "for years" after the crime.

Both Campbell and Red Robinson said they'd be willing to have Tracy Haynes of channel 5 come down and show them 1978 file footage to see if they could identify the vests. And Protess reported that Dennis Williams's lawyers were offering a $100 bounty for the first person who could come up with one of the vests.

As Protess rose to leave, Curt Robinson pulled him aside. He said that a couple of years after the crime he was smoking marijuana with Ira Johnson and "a Mexican guy." They'd described "what went down the night those white people got killed."

"The 'Mexican guy' was Johnny Rodriguez, right?" Protess interjected.

"Yeah, so you know?" Curt said.

"And I know there was a fourth guy involved, too."

Curt lowered his eyes, then slowly nodded. "I'm gonna write his name on a piece of paper," he said. "Maybe someday I'll give it to you."

■ ■ ■

As Marvin Simpson strolled home after dark, a car pulled alongside him. He increased his pace. So did the car. Simpson ran the remaining block, and the car peeled away.

The next weekend, two men approached him from behind on the street. One put a gun to the back of his neck and ordered him not to turn around.

"Keep talkin', mother-fucker," said the other, "and you're gonna get hurt."

■ ■ ■

David Protess called Rob Warden at the state's attorney's office in a panic, hoping something could be done to protect Marvin Simpson.

Warden thought it would be unwise to draw the office's attention to Simpson. In view of the threats Paula Gray had received, he said, state's attorney's investigators "would be more likely to harass him than protect him."

"Well we sure can't count on the Ford Heights cops or the sheriffs," Protess said.

The best thing to do, they agreed, was to keep Simpson's profile as low as possible for the time being.

"How's he holding up?" Warden asked.

"He's scared shitless, but he's hanging in there."

■ ■ ■

The students jetted to St. Louis on April 11, spending the night with Stacey Delo's parents before joining David Protess to interview Ira Johnson at Menard the next day.

Protess, a white-knuckle flyer, took his chances on Interstate 57, stopping at Danville to show Kenny Adams the street file. He found Adams in high spirits, delighted that Jeffrey Urdangen had agreed to represent him *pro bono* and that DNA testing had finally been approved.

Adams expressed concern, however, that DNA might not be detected on the eighteen-year-old vaginal swab and slide.

"Here's the back-up plan," said Protess, handing him the street file. "We'll prove who really did the crime."

Adams slowly read the document. Then he lowered his head, fighting back tears. "Why'd they hide this? Why? Why'd they do that?"

Protess took a long drag on a Carlton. "Look at the date in the top left corner."

"Seventeen May nineteen seventy-eight," Adams noted.

"A couple of days after the four of you had your first court appearance, when Judge McKay denied bond," said Protess. "The cops and prosecutors told the world they'd solved this horrible interracial crime."

"It was a circus," Adams recalled. "The media was everywhere—we was paraded before TV cameras like animals in a zoo."

"And the very next day, May the sixteenth, Paula told the grand jury that you guys did it," Protess observed.

Adams glanced again at the date on the street file. "So Marvin Simpson came along—"

"A day or two too late," Protess said. "They were already publicly committed to convicting you. And, with Paula's testimony, they were sure they could win."

"All for nothin'," Adams sighed. "All for nothin'."

Protess offered him a cigarette, but he declined.

"I quit," Adams said, his face brightening. "I'm preparin' for the day I might breathe free air, inhale those lake breezes again."

As a child, he explained, he'd found Lake Michigan a place to go to clear his head, a source of comfort whenever he felt anxious or confused. "Some deep breaths, and I'd be fine."

Adams asked what the lake looked like now.

Protess was embarrassed. He had to admit he hadn't paid much attention, even though the Northwestern campus overlooked it.

"Maybe we'll see it together soon," said Adams.

"If Ira Johnson tells the truth tomorrow," Protess said, "we will for sure."

■ ■ ■

Stephanie Goldstein and David Protess paced at the prison gate, awaiting word from inside.

The strategy was for Stacey Delo and Laura Sullivan to talk to Ira Johnson first. If all went according to plan, Goldstein and Protess would join in for the affidavit signing and picture taking.

After about half an hour, a guard informed Goldstein and Protess, "They'd like you to come in now."

Delo and Sullivan sat at a wobbly conference table opposite Johnson, who seemed bemused. A slender man just ten days short of his thirty-sixth birthday, he had a droopy left eye and was missing several teeth.

After introductions, Sullivan said, "Ira's done a good thing."

"What's that?" Protess asked Johnson.

"I told 'em what happened that night," he said. "My brother an' two other guys done the crime."

Protess asked if he'd put the details in writing.

Johnson nodded, and Delo handed him a legal pad and a pen. She sat to his right, to help with the wording and spelling.

Squinting, his face close to the page, Johnson wrote in a steady hand:

> The night of the murders I was in my room smoking pot when my brother Dennis walked in. He was acting real nervous. I asked Dennis, "What's up man?" He took a toke on the joint, and said, "I'm gonna tell you something, but you better not tell no mother-fucker."
>
> Dennis then admitted to me that he and two other men had just robbed a gas station in Homewood and stolen some money,

cigarettes, and beige-colored, white-wool-lined vests. He showed me the items he had taken.

At this time, Dennis also admitted that he and the other men had abducted "two honkies—a broad and a dude," driven them around about an hour in a Buick Electra 225, and taken them to a vacant apartment over by Deer Creek. Dennis told me that he and one of the other men had raped the woman, while the third man took the white guy to the creek. Dennis added that he shot the woman in the head and that he later learned that the man was shot twice by the creek.

Dennis told me that a .38-caliber revolver that belonged to me had been used in the crime. He'd told me when he borrowed my gun that he "was going to get some money." Dennis returned the .38 to me after committing the murder and I hid it under my mattress and sold it to Melvin Strayhorn the next day.

[T]he Buick Electra 225 used in the crime belonged to Johnny Rodriguez.

When Johnson finished writing, Protess read his statement over quickly and asked the names of the others involved in the crime.

"Donnell Griffin and Carl Richie," said Johnson.

"Who are they?" Protess asked, puzzled by the mention of two names he hadn't run across before.

"A couple of Disciples, associates of the Dude."

"Was Red Robinson involved?"

"Uh, no."

"How about Johnny Rodriguez? You say here that they used his car."

"Musta borrowed it."

Protess raised an eyebrow. "Are you willing to testify under oath to all this?" he asked.

"Yeah, I am," Johnson replied.

But he added that he didn't think prosecutors were interested in what he had to say.

He said he'd recently been visited by two men from the Markham branch of the state's attorney's office.

"They mentioned you and the girls by name," Johnson told Protess.

"What'd they say?"

"They said they'd get me moved to a better prison closer to home if I didn't tell you what I know about the crime."

Johnson said he'd rejected the offer. He thought it amusing that, until the visit from the two men from Markham, the authorities had never spoken with him about the crime.

After adding a paragraph about the offer to his written statement, Johnson signed and dated it.

"Now, how 'bout what you promised me?" Johnson asked.

The group went into the hall, where Goldstein snapped five Polaroid shots of Johnson flanked by Delo and Sullivan. For the final picture, Johnson put a hand on each student's shoulder as guards looked on disapprovingly.

In parting, Johnson asked the students, "Will you promise to write?"

They assured him they would.

The guards then quickly cuffed Johnson, seized the photos as contraband, and led him away, empty-handed.

14

Colloquies with Killers

▪ Channel 5 had two sensational stories, but Doug Longhini wasn't ready to run with either one.

In a videotaped interview with Tracy Haynes, Red Robinson had said the buckskin vest he'd "bought" from Dennis Johnson looked exactly like the one in the 1978 video from the Clark station.

And, on top of Ira Johnson's signed statement, a state's attorney's spokesperson had admitted to Longhini that two investigators had indeed visited Johnson before he'd talked to the Medill team. Although the spokesperson had refused to disclose the purpose of the visit, Longhini thought it smacked of yet another attempt to muzzle a witness who might discredit the original convictions.

Tempting as it was to go to air, Longhini concluded it was wiser to wait, concerned that more media heat might hamper the burgeoning investigation.

René Brown and David Protess were convinced that Robinson had been a participant in the crime—not just a buyer of a stolen vest—and wanted to take further cracks at interviewing him before he became publicly committed to his story. And Ira Johnson had come up with two new suspects, whom Brown and Protess hadn't yet investigated.

Longhini sensed that better stories lay ahead.

■ ■ ■

Poking around Ford Heights, René Brown soon discovered that Donnell Griffin and Carl Richie had shared Dennis Johnson's fate. Ira Johnson had pinned the crime on three dead gang-bangers.

Aside from the two new names, however, Johnson's scenario paralleled Marvin Simpson's. So Brown wanted to keep the dialogue with Johnson and Red Robinson going, hoping one or both would eventually tell the truth.

Brown focused on Robinson, thinking he might be susceptible to moral appeals. Unlike the Johnson brothers, Robinson had no criminal record. And, for years after the crime, he'd been seen by Marvin Simpson and others wandering aimlessly around the Heights, mumbling to himself, sometimes urinating in his pants.

Brown wanted to work on Robinson in a comfortable setting away from Ford Heights. Biamonte's Family Dining seemed perfect, cozy and quiet, dimly lit, with good food and cold beer, a place where Brown could do business.

It didn't take much to persuade Robinson to have a series of lunches there in April of 1996 to talk about the case—not as a suspect, but as a helpful source of information.

From time to time, David Protess or one of the students came along, too, and Brown always invited Marvin Simpson and David Campbell so Robinson would feel at ease.

Playing to Robinson's conscience, without ever addressing him directly, Brown mused that whoever committed the crime must be wracked with guilt. "How could they live with themselves, knowing an innocent brother is gonna be executed?" Brown wondered aloud.

He sprinkled his remarks with references to Scripture, speaking of the relief and redemption that only the truth could bring. Not only the killers knew the truth. God knew it, too.

Taking a slightly different approach, Brown observed, "Only a real man will ever own up to this crime."

The running commentary was punctuated occasionally by an "amen" from Simpson or Campbell.

Robinson said little, but continued to attend the lunches, listening intently.

As time passed, he slumped further into his seat.

■ ■ ■

Meanwhile, David Protess wrote Ira Johnson, asking him to call him at Northwestern concerning Donnell Griffin and Carl Richie.

Several days later, Johnson wrote back, saying the long-distance operators were refusing to put his calls through.

When Protess checked with Consolidated Communications, the company that provides phone service to prisons, he was told the Department of Corrections had put a block on calls to Protess's office "for unspecified reasons."

Exasperated, realizing it could take weeks of wrangling with bureaucrats to get the phone unblocked, Protess sent Johnson his home number.

But by the time Johnson received the letter and reached Protess, many days had lapsed—a delay that would prove propitious.

■ ■ ■

On May 8, René Brown and Jenner & Block's James Thompson were scrambling to get a last-minute affidavit from David Campbell for a motion due that week at the Illinois Supreme Court.

After Campbell signed, attesting that he'd heard the Johnson brothers planning a robbery on May 10, 1978, Brown asked Thompson if he needed anything else.

"It would be nice to have a confession from Red," Thompson said, facetiously.

"I'm gonna get him for you," said Brown.

Thompson just smiled and waved good-bye.

"Let's go see Moon," Brown told Campbell. They hopped in Campbell's car, picked up Marvin Simpson, and headed to Red Robinson's house.

He was in the yard, watering newly sown grass.

"Come on, let's hit Biamonte's," Brown suggested.

Robinson turned off the hose and climbed into the backseat, beside Simpson.

In a corner booth, after passing around Newports, Brown looked Robinson in the eye. "Let me tell you something, man," Brown said in a steady voice. "You need to talk. Today's the day."

"Could I have a beer?" Red asked.

"Sure," said Brown, who ordered one for everybody but himself.

"You know what, man, I know you're about to tell me some more things I need to know," Brown continued. "I want you to relax and talk. We're here together with people you've been around all your life."

Simpson and Campbell nodded supportively.

Robinson took a swig of Bud and a long drag from a Newport.

"I was there," he sighed.

On the evening of May 10, Robinson said, he'd been drinking beer under the old oak tree with Simpson, Campbell, and Johnny Rodriguez when Dennis and Ira Johnson arrived.

Dennis asked Johnny to drive him to get some money at a Homewood filling station, and Johnny agreed. "I didn't want to go with them," said Robinson, "but Dennis put a gun on me."

At the station, Dennis went inside and quickly returned, saying, "Them motherfuckers ain't got my money." He went back with a pistol and brought two white people out, putting the girl in the front and the guy in the back of Johnny's Buick Electra. Ira loaded some vests and cartons of cigarettes into the trunk.

"We went to that townhouse, but didn't stay 'cause there was people around," Robinson continued. "So we drove around for 'bout an hour and come back."

Johnny waited in the car, while everyone else went inside. Then Dennis and Ira took turns raping the white girl. "The last time I seen her she was on her knees, and Dennis shot her in the head. I ran on outta there. I ran all the way home."

The next morning, Robinson said, he bought one of the vests from Dennis for ten dollars.

"That's all I know," he said, finishing his beer.

Brown didn't believe it *was* all Robinson knew, but thought it was good enough for the time being.

"A burden is off your shoulders," said Brown, adding that it would "help save Dennis Williams's life" if Robinson would put what he'd said in writing.

He agreed, but said he couldn't draft it himself.

Just then, Laura Sullivan and Stephanie Goldstein arrived.

They were not happy. They'd been assigned to interview Melvin Strayhorn, who'd purportedly purchased the murder weapon from Ira Johnson. Brown was supposed to have met them at Marvin Simpson's house to pursue the Strayhorn interview, but they'd been stood up. Now they'd found Brown in a bar.

"Red's got something to tell you," Brown said.

Sullivan indignantly reminded him that they were supposed to be looking for Strayhorn.

"This'll be better," Brown assured her.

After some discussion about whether David Protess should be called to mediate the matter, Sullivan and Goldstein decided to hear whatever it was that Robinson had to say.

The students were stunned.

Grabbing a school notebook, Sullivan hastily summarized Robinson's statement, and the group went to a currency exchange, where he signed the four-page document before a notary.

Brown and the students then went to see Strayhorn, who claimed he didn't recall buying a .38 from Ira.

Afterward, Sullivan called Protess.

"Melvin Strayhorn didn't tell us anything," she reported, "but, guess what?"

"What?" he asked.

"We got Red Robinson to confess."

■ ■ ■

Two days later at Biamonte's, Red Robinson played to a larger crowd.

He repeated his story to Eric Zorn, Tracy Haynes, Doug Longhini, a channel 5 cameraman, David Protess, Stephanie Goldstein, René Brown, and a smattering of curious customers.

The event broke the dike at channel 5, which unleashed a barrage of stories, publicly identifying the alternative suspects for the first time and questioning why the authorities had failed even to interview them eighteen years earlier.

In the *Tribune*, Zorn put the state's attorney's office on notice: "Responsibility for this case now belongs to Jack O'Malley. If a handful of journalists and college kids beat him to the truth, he risks taking blame, not receiving credit, when justice is finally done."

■ ■ ■

"An overwhelming body of newly discovered evidence strongly suggests that Dennis Williams has spent eighteen years of his life on Death Row for a crime he did not commit," Robert Byman wrote in his motion to the Illinois Supreme Court.

"An innocent man faces execution, having had his postconviction petition dismissed without a hearing," the motion said. "This case should be remanded to the trial court for further proceedings in light of the new evidence."

Attached to the motion were the street file and affidavits by Paula Gray, Red Robinson, Ira Johnson, Marvin Simpson, George Nance, and David Campbell, among others.

The motion also was accompanied by a surprise affidavit by Byman himself, saying: "Within the last week, I have learned that Dr. David Bing has found testable DNA from the semen of a person or persons who had sex with Carol Schmal shortly before she was murdered."

Bing was still awaiting blood and saliva samples from Williams and his codefendants and, after he received them, he expected it would take two or three weeks to compare their DNA with that from the swab and slide, the affidavit said.

It added, charitably, that the state's attorney's office had been fully cooperating in the testing.

■ ■ ■

In the wake of the media frenzy following Red Robinson's press conference, the state's attorney's office could hardly oppose Robert Byman's motion without looking worse than it already did.

Rob Warden's only lament, he told Byman, was that the office didn't have the good sense to join in his request for a hearing in the trial court.

But at least prosecutors were no longer standing in the way of justice, and the same pressures that had forced them to retreat would now be exerted on the justices of the supreme court.

■ ■ ■

"Ira, cut the bullshit," David Protess said when Ira Johnson finally called on May 14. "Donnell Griffin and Carl Richie weren't involved."

"Well, you know—" Johnson stammered.

"And Red Robinson *was*," Protess interrupted. "He confessed to us last week."

"Red was there?" Johnson said with mock surprise.

"Yeah, and he says you were, too. He says *you* raped the girl."

Protess sensed that Johnson was burning.

"So I be protectin' him, an' he goes ahead an' does me," said Johnson. "He ain't tellin' ya the truth. I didn't rape nobody."

"Are you ready to tell the truth now?"

"Send Stacey and Laura down. I'll tell 'em everything, but Red ain't gonna like it."

Johnson placed one, nonnegotiable condition on the interview: "We're gonna talk in the visiting area."

"If Stacey and Laura say it's okay," Protess told him, "it's okay with me."

■ ■ ■

"Why's he so insistent on the visiting area?" Stacey Delo asked the next day.

Protess wasn't sure. "Maybe he wants to show you off, or maybe he knows you can't take notes or tape-record him there," he speculated. "And we're gonna have to give him your last names so he can put you on his visitors' list."

Whatever Johnson's intent, Delo and Laura Sullivan were wary. But, not wanting to risk losing the interview, they'd do it on his terms.

On the eve of the trip, their trepidation wasn't exactly allayed when David Protess cautioned them: "Don't go near a washroom—he could drag you in—and sit as close as you can to the guards."

When they arrived on May 20, the room was filled with prisoners, their wives, friends, and children. Although the scene was chaotic, the presence of the young women sitting with Johnson immediately caught the attention of two guards.

A glint of recognition crossed the guards' faces, and one stalked off just as the interview began.

Ira Johnson, fortunately, wasted no time in admitting that he'd been present for the entire crime.

"Dennis wanted to do a score, an' asked me to come along," he said. "He didn't have a car, so he paid Johnny to drive his deuce and a quarter, an' Red just jumped in.

"When we got to the gas station, Dennis took the girl 'cause he liked the way she looked—know what I'm sayin'?—an' he took the boyfriend 'cause he couldn't leave no witnesses.

"We drove around an' went to the townhouse. I seen Dennis rape her. An' Red did her, too. But me an' Johnny didn't touch the girl. Then Dennis makes me an' Johnny take the boyfriend out to the creek an' get rid of him."

"You're saying you shot Larry Lionberg?" Sullivan asked.

"Yeah, I—" He was interrupted by a guard.

"You're going to have to leave," the guard informed Delo and Sullivan.

"But—" Sullivan started to protest.

"Now!" said the guard, taking both her and Delo by the arm.

They were escorted from the prison—accused of pretending to be just visitors when they really were there for an interview—and informed they wouldn't be welcome back.

■ ■ ■

"We got kicked out of the prison," Stacey Delo shrieked from her car phone. "They practically carried us out."

As she rambled on about the circumstances, David Protess assured her that he'd try to straighten out the misunderstanding with the Department of Corrections.

"Did Ira get to tell you anything?" he finally asked.

"Oh, yeah," Delo said. "He admitted killing Larry Lionberg."

"Holy shit, Stacey—you buried the lead!" Protess exclaimed. "Write down everything you can remember him saying. Go to your parents' house. And I'll work on getting you back in the prison."

■ ■ ■

David Protess pleaded the students' case to Nic Howell, the Illinois Department of Corrections spokesperson, and Charles Hinsley, the assistant warden at Menard.

"You can't be a journalist one day and a regular visitor another day," Hinsley declared. "Besides, I've got those pictures they took a couple of weeks ago. I think they were inappropriate."

"But they didn't deceive anyone," Protess insisted. "Their names were on the approved visitors' list, and you let the camera in. They took the pictures right in front of the guards, for God's sake."

Hinsley wouldn't budge.

Stacey Delo and Laura Sullivan were permanently barred from all Illinois prisons.

Protess told the disheartened pair to return to the campus.

The next morning, Ira Johnson reached Protess at home.

Furious at the authorities, Johnson agreed to see Protess and Stephanie Goldstein, as journalists, in the conference room.

■ ■ ■

Charles Hinsley wasn't about to make it easy to interview Ira Johnson.

When David Protess sought permission for him and Stephanie Goldstein to do the interview, Hinsley said he'd barred her, too. Her offense had been seeing Dennis Williams as a regular visitor and Ira Johnson as a journalist.

"She can't be both," said Hinsley.

Protess said she'd shown her student ID before visiting Williams.

"Doesn't matter."

Hinsley said Protess could interview Johnson. But if Protess tape-recorded the interview, Hinsley would have to hear the tape. "Then, I'll decide if you can take it with you," he declared.

"Whatever," Protess said.

On May 29, Protess drove to St. Louis. His wife, Joan, went along, hoping to meet Dennis Williams the next day while her husband interviewed Johnson. When they checked into the hotel, there was an urgent message to call Jenner & Block's James Thompson at home.

"Great news!" Thompson reported. "The supreme court granted our motion. They ordered a hearing on the new evidence."

Thompson read the one-paragraph order and authorized Joan Protess to deliver the news to Williams in person.

After calling the students and Williams's brother, James, the Protesses strolled along the riverfront under the St. Louis arch.

It was a clear, starry night, and fragrances of spring filled the air.

■ ■ ■

Stooped over, weighted down by leg irons and handcuffs, Dennis Williams simply shrugged when Joan Protess told him of the previous day's supreme court order.

The supreme court had given him hope once before—fourteen years ago—and look where it had gotten him.

He'd just been moved, with the rest of his condemned cohorts, into the Pit, where the cells were smaller and the food worse. The prisoners were boycotting outdoor recreation, a protest Williams had joined but didn't care to lead.

"The only court order that will ever lift my spirits," he said, "is the one that sets me free."

And he doubted he'd live to see such an order, convinced as he was that prosecutors would stop at nothing—even rigging the DNA results—to ensure his execution.

■ ■ ■

While Joan Protess was trying to cheer up Dennis Williams, her husband was with the man who'd actually murdered Larry Lionberg.

"This is from Stacey," David Protess said, handing Ira Johnson a sealed envelope.

It contained a handwritten letter, in which Delo said that although she'd been horrified by his admissions she considered him a "hero" for finally telling the truth and helping exonerate four innocent men.

Johnson read the letter, silently moving his lips. He smiled and stuffed it into his pants pocket.

Then Protess gave him an affidavit summarizing what Johnson had told the students before their ejection from Menard.

"Are they gonna kill me if I sign this?" Johnson asked.

"Can't imagine that," said Protess, explaining that never in Illinois history had anyone been prosecuted for a murder in which someone else had been wrongly convicted. "The state just doesn't admit mistakes like this. It's too embarrassing."

But, in the unlikely event that the prosecutors broke precedent, Protess promised, "I'll get you the best lawyer I can find."

Johnson studied Protess.

"I'm gonna trust you," Johnson said. "I can't see them four innocent guys, you know, doin' any more time."

"You're doin' the right thing, Ira," said Protess. "I'll go find the prison notary."

"How 'bout gettin' me a pizza and a Sprite?" Johnson asked.

Protess filled the order at the commissary and returned with the food and the notary.

After Johnson signed the affidavit, Protess asked him to briefly describe the crime on tape for channel 5.

"We went to this Homewood filling station to get some gas," Johnson said. "Dennis demanded us to rob the place. 'We're gonna take the guy an' the girl with us,' he said."

After Dennis—and Red—raped Carol Schmal in the abandoned

townhouse, Johnson continued, "I heard shots an' Red ran outta there.

"Then Dennis told me and Johnny to take the white guy over there by the creek. 'You better shoot him,' he said. 'You're gonna shoot him.' I didn't want him to shoot me. I know what he was capable of.

"So I shot the guy in the head."

Asked if Dennis knew the victims, Johnson replied, "No, man, they was just in the wrong place at the wrong time."

As Protess turned off the tape recorder, preparing to leave, Johnson said, "You wanna know somethin' strange, man?"

"What's that?"

"When we was ridin' around with the guy an' the girl, there was a song playin' on the radio that was real popular back then. I've never forgot that. It was called 'Stayin' Alive.' "

■ ■ ■

Pushing the play button on Protess's recorder, Charles Hinsley leaned back in his chair.

He grimaced as he listened.

When the tape ended, he asked, "Anything on the other side?"

"You've heard all of it," Protess assured him.

"What troubles me," Hinsley said, "it that this pertains to one of our other prisoners, Dennis Williams."

"He won't be one of your other prisoners much longer," Protess said. "You don't want to stand in the way of that happening, do you?"

Hinsley returned the recorder. "Have a nice day," he said.

Protess got out while the getting was good.

■ ■ ■

At speeds approaching a hundred miles an hour, David and Joan Protess shot up the interstate.

Channel 5 investigative reporter Dave Savini, who'd taken over the story while Tracy Haynes was on vacation, met them at an Oak Park baseball diamond, where they arrived in the nick of time for Protess to manage their son Benji's Little League game.

Protess handed Savini the tape and did an interview at the edge of left field with game action in the background.

The story, featuring Ira Johnson's sound bites and pictures of the murder victims, led that night's ten o'clock news.

Live in the newsroom, Savini branded the police investigation of the murders "botched from the very beginning."

■ ■ ■

State's attorney's investigators descended on Ford Heights the next day, May 31.

Of all those they wanted to interview, the only one they could find was Johnny Rodriguez, whom they took to Markham for questioning.

Rodriguez, now thirty-six years old, readily admitted that his Buick Electra had been used in the crime. He claimed, however, that he'd passed out drunk in the backseat and knew nothing until he awoke to find a white woman sitting between him and Dennis Johnson. A white man was between Red Robinson and Ira Johnson in the front seat.

When they'd arrived at the abandoned townhouse, he said, someone threw him his car keys, and he drove home.

Asked if he could identify the woman, he said, "I saw her picture on channel 5 last night."

The investigators took Rodriguez back to Ford Heights, assuring him they'd be in touch.

15

The Blood Cries Out

▪ In the waning days of May 1996, the action in the case shifted to the sterile confines of Dr. David Bing's state-of-the-art laboratory in Boston.

The tall, graying Harvard professor was beginning the painstaking task of comparing the DNA isolated from the swab and slide with that extracted from the defendants' fresh blood samples.

He subjected the material from the swab and slide to DQ alpha typing, a PCR-based technique that zeroes in on a region of the sixth chromosome rich with distinctive characteristics. In addition, he performed a polymarker PCR test, which focuses on several other genetic regions.

The tests identified a genetic pattern that is present in about one in a thousand African-American men and far fewer Caucasian men.

The question was whether that pattern also was present in any of the defendants' blood, which Bing subjected to conventional DNA testing known as RFLP (restriction fragment length polymorphism).

Bing first compared Dennis Williams's DNA, then Kenny Adams's, then Verneal Jimerson's, and finally Willie Rainge's.

One after another, he found no match.

It was an historic result: the first time in the annals of forensic science that multiple defendants had been excluded as sources of semen in a rape case.

■ ■ ■

Jack O'Malley summoned his three top prosecutors to an emergency meeting in his office when Dr. Bing faxed his findings on June 6.

"What do we do now?" the state's attorney asked First Assistant Andrea Zopp, Criminal Prosecutions Chief John Eannace, and Felony Trial Division Chief Scott Nelson.

The only thing they knew for sure was that *something* had to be done fast, preferably before Eric Zorn and channel 5 started demanding comment.

If they delayed, the O'Malley administration would surely be portrayed as stonewalling in the face of a terrible injustice.

But they weren't ready to admit that the Ford Heights Four were innocent.

For one thing, David Bing's findings didn't preclude a scenario, however unlikely, under which they might be guilty: Perhaps the rapists hadn't ejaculated and the semen was Larry Lionberg's.

Although Lionberg had been ruled out by Michael Podlecki, the state's expert at the 1978 trial, Podlecki could have been wrong. He'd certainly been wrong about other things, including Dennis Williams's secretor status.

The prosecutors were of one mind that the office should do nothing drastic until Bing tested hair samples of Lionberg's that had been preserved.

For another thing, Zopp in particular was concerned about the impact that admitting the mistake could have on the victims' families. She wanted time to explain the new developments.

Finally, she wanted state's attorney's investigators to thoroughly check out the alternative suspects. Were they telling the truth? David Protess, she thought, might be pulling a public relations stunt. But if he weren't, it would be ideal to charge the real killers at the same time the innocent men were released.

Still, the media were circling like sharks and had to be fed.

Since DNA had been the only hope of reconvicting Verneal Jimerson, it seemed to make sense to announce immediately that the charges against him would be dropped and that the other defendants' cases would be taken under advisement.

■ ■ ■

After drafting a brief statement, Jack O'Malley called Rob Warden at home.

"Oh, no, don't release that," cautioned Warden, who'd been apprised of the DNA results by David Protess.

Warden contended that dropping one case and not the others would look inconsistent. "Either they're all guilty, or they're all innocent—and now the answer is clear."

"You're probably right," O'Malley said, "but we can't say that yet."

"Then don't say anything."

Warden assured him that the story wouldn't break for at least a day. Protess had shared the DNA results with Eric Zorn and Doug Longhini, but on the condition that they'd do nothing until the defense lawyers caucused the next afternoon.

"Let me get Protess in to meet with you and Zopp in the morning," Warden said. "You should at least hear what he's got on the other suspects before you issue a statement."

O'Malley agreed.

■ ■ ■

Dennis Williams called David Protess that night, sounding beaten down.

"Hope I didn't interrupt your dinner," Williams began.

"Dennis, don't you *know*?"

"Know what?"

"You're exonerated! The DNA came back. It clears *all* of you."

"What? You mean they didn't rig it?"

"It was legit, and it's only a matter of time now until you're free."

"Oh, man! Oh, man! Oh, man!"

Williams dropped the phone.

"Dennis, are you okay?" Protess shouted.

He could hear sobbing on the other end.

Muffled at first, the sobs soon grew louder, a catharsis after eighteen years of agony.

■ ■ ■

Dennis Williams turned on his homemade boombox and inserted an eight-track tape he'd had a long time, but hadn't wanted to hear.

It was "Stop That Train" by Bob Marley and the Wailers.

The reggae music resonated through the prison gallery:

Stop that train, I'm leaving
Stop that train, I'm leaving
It won't be too long
It won't be too long
*Stop that train, I'm leaving.**

■ ■ ■

The next morning, June 7, Andrea Zopp grilled David Protess in her office for almost an hour while Rob Warden made nervous chitchat with Jack O'Malley next door.

Assuming that Protess saw the state's attorney's office as the en-

*"Stop That Train" written by Peter Tosh. Copyright 1972 by Fifty-Six Hope Road Music, Ltd. Used by permission. All rights reserved.

emy, Zopp expected him to be guarded. But he immediately turned over all the affidavits and tape recordings he had pertaining to the alternate suspects. "You can have everything I've shared with the defense lawyers," he assured her. "I'll cooperate fully."

Zopp asked pointed questions about how the information had been obtained, focusing on Ira Johnson's admission that he'd shot Larry Lionberg.

Aware of Protess's opposition to the death penalty, she tried to rattle him by saying of Johnson, "If what you're telling me is true, we're gonna kill him."

Protess didn't flinch. There'd be time to argue later.

Zopp rose and shook his hand. "I look forward to working with you and meeting your students. It must have been an incredible experience for them."

Excusing herself momentarily, she went into O'Malley's office and looked directly at Rob Warden.

"I hate it when you're right," she said.

Warden and O'Malley laughed.

Zopp returned to her office with O'Malley, who asked Protess to invite the defense team to come to the state's attorney's office for a meeting as soon as possible.

"They're getting together this afternoon at Jenner and Block. I think they'll be willing to come over here."

Protess called Robert Byman, who said it would be fine with him, but thought it was too late to reach the others. He'd have to wait until they arrived at 2:00 P.M.

The meeting at Jenner & Block lasted about thirty seconds. As soon as Protess extended O'Malley's invitation, Byman asked, "What are we waiting for?"

The group descended on the Daley Center at 2:15.

"This is certainly an unusual situation," O'Malley told them. "What do you suggest we do?"

"How about joining us in a motion to immediately dismiss all the charges against all the defendants?" suggested Jeffrey Urdangen, Kenny Adams's lawyer.

After a tense pause, Zopp broke the silence. "Hey, it never hurts to ask."

While the office was prepared to drop the Jimerson case, Zopp said a decision on the other three cases would be deferred until additional DNA tests were completed, in light of the possibility that the semen was Lionberg's.

"That's not a realistic possibility," said Matthew Kennelly, one of Willie Rainge's lawyers, pointing out that Dr. Bing was virtually certain the semen hadn't come from a Caucasian.

"We've still got to rule Lionberg out," said O'Malley. "It should only take a couple of weeks."

Rainge's other lawyer, Lawrence Marshall, asked if the state's attorney's office would agree to release the men on electronic home monitoring in the meantime.

Marshall was expecting another "hey it never hurts to ask" response, but O'Malley didn't hesitate.

"Sure," he said.

The air went out of the room.

Warden and Protess exchanged glances, tears welling in their eyes.

The men were finally coming home.

Struggling to compose himself, Protess asked if the home monitoring would allow the men to go outside. "These guys have spent half their lives in cages," he said.

The prosecutors promised to see if the transmitting devices could be positioned to allow that.

One problem remained: getting the cases of the three defendants still in prison before a judge who could effect their release. O'Malley suggested consolidating the cases before Thomas Fitzgerald, presiding judge of the Cook County Criminal Courts.

When the defense lawyers agreed, Felony Trial Division Chief

Scott Nelson called Fitzgerald, who set a hearing seven days hence, on June 14.

Before then, the defense lawyers would have to find suitable places for the men to live. And O'Malley agreed to intercede with the Department of Corrections to have Willie Rainge moved into an area of Pontiac where he'd be safe.

"Nobody has said this yet, but we appreciate your prompt way of handling this," Robert Byman told O'Malley.

Marshall added, "The issue is not whether mistakes were made, but how they are addressed when they are discovered."

O'Malley thanked them, sighing, "I hope eighteen years from now no one discovers that anything like this happened on my watch."

■ ■ ■

After celebratory drinks at a Loop tavern, Mark Ter Molen and David Protess took a cab to channel 5 while Rob Warden drafted a statement on behalf of the state's attorney's office.

Ter Molen said on camera: "The DNA evidence establishes that the four men are all innocent. It is an amazing miscarriage of justice."

The official statement said: "The state's attorney's office will review all of the new evidence and take appropriate action in the interest of justice as quickly as possible."

And channel 5 added its own spin: "Our four-month unit five investigation uncovered allegations of a botched police investigation, allegations of a forced confession, and we also uncovered the secret police files that were buried for years."

■ ■ ■

There was no shortage of offers of shelter from relatives of Dennis Williams, Kenny Adams, and Willie Rainge, but a few family squabbles arose over who would stay where. The situation called for diplomacy, a skill the men had perfected in prison.

Not wanting to hurt any feelings, they made the decisions, and blamed their lawyers.

Williams would stay with his brother, James, and sister-in-law, Vella, in the Beverly neighborhood of Chicago—the home where Dennis Johnson had first admitted his involvement in the crime.

Adams would stay with his older brother, Billy, in south suburban Matteson, not far from their elderly mother's home in Ford Heights.

Rainge would stay with his wheelchair-bound son, Tederol, in a federally subsidized townhouse in southwest suburban Orland Hills.

Verneal Jimerson, meanwhile, had no choice about his living arrangements. He'd recently tested positive in routine drug screening by the sheriff's office, and Judge Sheila Murphy had sent him to a halfway house.

His living situation wouldn't be resolved until at least June 24, the date of his next hearing before Murphy. Then he could live where he pleased—if prosecutors kept their promise to drop the murder case.

16

A Whole New World

FRIDAY, JUNE 14, 1996

As a fleeting stillness settled over the Condemned Unit at Menard, prisoner A63823 methodically packed his worldly belongings into a cardboard box. Sealing it with masking tape, he scrawled his brother's name and address across the top with a black felt marker.

He turned, gestured for a guard to cuff his hands, and was led away, clutching the marker, a few sheets of blank paper, and a photograph of his mother.

Walking past sleeping prisoners, he paused to pray for their souls.

A few yards further and the prison gate swung open.

Peering into the darkness, he saw the vehicle that awaited him—not the sleek sedan from his dream, but a prison van. No matter, if it got him where he longed to go.

Dennis Williams glanced behind him and strode into the moonlit night for his long ride to freedom.

■ ■ ■

Shortly after 9:00 A.M., three childhood friends embraced in a basement lockup of the Cook County Jail, encumbered only by the chains that bound their hands.

They had just moments to talk before their lawyers arrived, time enough to share their fears. Would some last-minute trick block their release? Would they be welcome in a world that had passed them by?

Soon it would be time to find out.

Guards led the group through a tunnel and up an elevator to Judge Thomas Fitzgerald's first-floor courtroom, which was packed with family, friends, and reporters. David and Joan Protess were in the front row with their son, Benji. Behind them were the three students and René Brown, all four accompanied by their mothers.

As the prosecutors, defendants, and their cadre of counsel approached the bench, Dennis Williams turned and winked.

The hearing was perfunctory.

Thumbing through papers, Fitzgerald said he'd received motions to release the men on electronic home monitoring. Andrea Zopp said the state had no objection, and Fitzgerald signed the order.

"Your honor, I have an unusual request at this time," said Robert Byman. "Would it be possible for the men to attend the Medill graduation tomorrow afternoon? It would mean a lot to them and to the students."

Fitzgerald had anticipated Byman's request because that morning's Eric Zorn column, headlined "Students' legwork went further than long arm of law," mentioned that the men wanted to attend the ceremony to show their gratitude.

"I can't allow that," said the jurist, contending it would unduly burden the correctional officers in charge of home monitoring.

Looking down from the bench, Fitzgerald sternly warned the men, "It's going to be very tempting for you to break the rules after all these years, and I urge you not to do so. Do you understand?"

They nodded, silently suffering the gratuitous admonition.

Fitzgerald scheduled another hearing for July 2, allowing time to finish both the DNA testing and the investigation of the alternative suspects.

As the men were escorted from the courtroom, Dennis Williams's eyes met Joan Protess's. He triumphantly thrust his arms into the air, clanging his chains resoundingly.

A few minutes later, in a back room, the chains were exchanged for electronic ankle bracelets.

The men said good-bye to each other and then, in a touch of irony dictated by procedure, sheriff's deputies drove them home.

■ ■ ■

At 1:15 P.M., Dennis Williams stepped out of an unmarked white patrol car and into David Protess's arms.

"You look great!" said Protess. "How do you feel?"

"Well, in the words of Arnold Schwarzenegger, I'm back."

James and Vella Williams's two-story brick bungalow was decorated with yellow balloons for the homecoming and a yellow ribbon adorned a chrome sculpture of an eagle on the lawn.

As soon as the sheriffs left, Dennis ambled into the expansive backyard where a dozen or so well-wishers awaited him with freshly fried chicken, cold beer, and hand-packed ice cream.

After several helpings of each, Dennis toyed with Protess's remote-control car alarm and Byman's palm-sized cellular phone with amazement. "I feel like Rip Van Winkle," he said.

James Williams arrived a couple of hours later, in his Greyhound bus driver's uniform, just back from a Des Moines run. Tearfully hugging his brother, he exclaimed, "Is this for real, or are you a ghost?"

"I dunno, bro, I'm pretty numb," said Dennis.

"We're gonna bring ya back to life," James assured him. "You're gonna get a lot of love here."

As the sun set and the leaves rustled in a gentle breeze, the brothers sat at a picnic table, sipping beer, recalling good times from a distant past.

■ ■ ■

In brother Billy's recreation room, Kenny Adams was swarmed by nieces and nephews he'd never seen and a baby brother who'd just turned twenty-one.

Several young women from the south suburban neighborhood were there, flirting unabashedly with the handsome guest of honor.

But Kenny seemed too tired and distracted to enjoy the attention. He paced, pausing now and then to tug at the heavy device locked to his ankle.

"Is it bothering you?" his sister, Juanita, asked.

"It's my slave bracelet," he answered. "After all this time, I shouldn't be tied to nothin' no more."

To make matters worse, the sheriffs had inexplicably set the alarm so that he couldn't go outside.

He rubbed his hand across his freshly shaven head and looked down, wondering if he'd ever be truly free.

Claudette Adams noticed. Putting her arms around his broad shoulders, she comforted him with a mother's love.

Kenny sank into an easy chair and wanly smiled.

■ ■ ■

Willie Rainge sat at the bedside of his son, Tederol, mopping his brow with a cold washcloth.

The gunshot wound that had crippled Tederol two years earlier had never healed and was now infected, causing a raging fever.

The last time Willie had tended to his son had been to change his diaper. Now he changed the dressing on the gaping hole in his back.

Heavy doses of Tylenol and antibiotics finally broke the fever.

"You're gonna be okay," Willie reassured him. "Your daddy's with you now."

Father and son talked until daybreak about a trip they'd take someday to a faraway place where there'd be no pain.

SATURDAY, JUNE 15, 1996

"Three Innocent of Killing Go Free, Thanks to Students and DNA," said a front-page headline in the *New York Times* on commencement morning.

Network TV crews descended on the Evanston campus to capture every step and word of Stacey Delo, Stephanie Goldstein, and Laura Sullivan.

"The cameras are here because special congratulations are in order for three of our graduating seniors and Professor David Protess," Medill Dean Michael Janeway explained at the beginning of the ceremony. "What they did is in the best tradition of investigative reporting."

The crowd of more than a thousand cheered.

And the cheering resumed, louder than before, as each of the three received her diploma, followed by a hug from Protess.

Outside on the lawn, the students responded to reporters' queries about their futures. Delo would produce educational videos for children's television. Goldstein would take a summer job at Jenner & Block and enter law school in the fall. And Sullivan would be a reporting intern for New York *Newsday*.

"They are journalism students with an education in life and death and injustice," ABC correspondent Erin Hayes reported that evening.

The camera cut to Protess saying, "I'm very proud of them, and they all got *A*s."

"Well," Hayes concluded, "they certainly did their homework."

■ ■ ■

While the stars of the Medill class of '96 were doing interviews in Evanston, Arthur "Red" Robinson was doing one in Markham.

Robinson's interviewer was John Eannace, chief of criminal prosecutions for the state's attorney's office.

After Eannace read him his rights, Robinson admitted for the first time that he'd been a willing participant in the crime, providing the following account.

He, the Johnson brothers, and Johnny Rodriguez left the projects in the early morning hours of May 11, 1978, in Rodriguez's Buick Electra.

When Rodriguez pulled into the station for gas, Dennis Johnson went inside and started talking to the white couple. Suddenly, he pulled out a long-barrel .38 and frisked them.

Ira Johnson ran inside and returned to the car with some vests and cartons of cigarettes. Robinson helped carry out more loot, all of which was put into the trunk of Rodriguez's car.

Dennis Johnson then emerged with the couple, who clung to each other. At gunpoint, he ordered the woman into the front seat next to Johnny and the man into the back next to Robinson. When the man protested, Johnson pistol-whipped him.

They drove around for more than an hour—Rodriguez was at the wheel—before arriving at the townhouse. All six got out and went inside.

"What are you gonna do to us?" the woman asked.

"We're gonna have sex with you," Dennis Johnson answered.

Johnson and Robinson took her upstairs, where Johnson forced her to take off her clothes and raped her.

"Please don't kill me," she pleaded.

"Shut up, bitch," he said, placing the gun to her head and firing twice.

Robinson then ran out of the townhouse, past Rodriguez and Ira Johnson, who were holding the white man at gunpoint on the first floor.

As he fled, he heard two more shots.

■ ■ ■

Red Robinson's statement put prosecutors in a bind.

They couldn't charge him with the crime unless they acknowledged the innocence of the four men originally convicted, which they weren't prepared to do until at least July 2.

So they arranged to take Robinson's blood for DNA analysis and released him, ordering state's attorney's investigators to keep an eye on him.

Meanwhile, investigators interviewed Robinson's mother, Dorothy, and brother, Curt.

Dorothy acknowledged that Red had once owned a brown vest that "he got from one of the Johnson boys and wore for a long time." Several years ago, she'd started a fire to keep mosquitoes away and "threw in the vest."

Curt said that "in the summer of 1978" he'd seen Red, Ira, Dennis, and Johnny sitting in Johnny's Buick Electra. When Curt asked what was up, Ira told him, "We just killed two honkies."

■ ■ ■

It didn't take long for family friction to build in the Williams household.

Dennis wasn't picking up his clothes, wasn't emptying his ashtrays, and wasn't taking off his shoes before walking on the plush, cream carpeting in the living room.

Vella intended to enforce the house rules, and Dennis was sick of rules.

On his third day of restricted freedom, a loud argument broke out between Vella and her daughter over nothing of consequence.

Dennis covered his ears with his hands, leaped to his feet, and declared he'd rather be in the county jail.

Heading for the front door, he was intercepted by James, who prevented him from leaving but couldn't calm him down.

After a few minutes of ranting, Dennis grabbed the phone. He called Kenny Adams.

"I didn't do eighteen years to end up like this," he screamed. "I'm outta here, and the sheriffs can try to find me."

Adams's voice was soothing.

"Man, I know what you're dealin' with," he said. "But we been through a lot worse than this. You can't quit now. That's just what the cops want."

As they talked, Dennis realized that any rash act on his part would reflect on Kenny and the others.

"You're right, man," he said sheepishly. "You stayed strong for me all these years, an' now I'll stay strong for you."

MONDAY, JUNE 24, 1996

Wearing a tight-fitting, three-piece polyester suit, Verneal Jimerson sat at the defense table in Judge Sheila Murphy's courtroom and waited, chewing the cuticle of his right index finger.

He'd been patient for eleven years. And now, at age forty-three, the prosecutors wanted him to wait even longer. Mark Ter Molen had told him that Andrea Zopp, who was already more than an hour late for the hearing, would ask for another continuance.

Zopp wanted Jimerson's case heard with the others on July 2, he'd been told, which meant placing his fate in the hands of Judge Thomas Fitzgerald.

But Sheila Murphy was the only judge Jimerson trusted. She'd freed him on bond and then, when he'd disappointed her by flunking a drug test, denied a request by prosecutors to put him back in jail.

He'd pleased her by staying clean and becoming a teacher at the halfway house.

Jimerson was confident he'd get justice from Murphy and hoped today would be the day.

Suddenly, there was a whirlwind of activity as Zopp breezed into the courtroom, dressed in the color purple.

Murphy smiled thinly. "It's a pleasure to have the first assistant appearing in Markham," she said. "We don't often get that pleasure."

"I apologize for the delay," said Zopp, who was perspiring. "It was my fault. I don't get out here too often. It took me a while."

"Not a problem," said Murphy.

Zopp asked Murphy to hold off ruling on Ter Molen's motion to drop all charges, saying the state's attorney's office wasn't ready to admit that Jimerson had been wrongly convicted.

"The DNA evidence, while it certainly weakens our case, does not establish that Mr. Jimerson didn't do it," she contended. "It certainly requires us to do what we are doing," she said: more testing and investigating "whether other people committed this offense."

Zopp argued that any hearing on the new evidence at this point would "jeopardize the ongoing investigation" into the other suspects.

"We need just a little more time," she concluded.

"I'd like to bring the focus back to Mr. Verneal Jimerson because he is why we are here today," Ter Molen countered. "He would like to have this cloud taken away from over his head and return to his life."

Ter Molen said he "heartily commended" the state for reopening the investigation, adding, however, that the case against Jimerson already was so weak that it should be dropped immediately.

Addressing Zopp, Murphy said, "I cannot allow you to dictate to the court when a hearing should proceed. You are a separate branch of government, and you understand that better than anyone."

"Yes, I do—" said Zopp.

Murphy interrupted, addressing the defendant: "Mr. Jimerson, your case involved a separate trial in 1985, and it's not in the interest of justice to consolidate these cases, so we'll continue with the hearing right now."

"Thank you, your honor," said Ter Molen, as Jimerson smiled.

Murphy then asked Ter Molen to explain why Jimerson should go free.

Ter Molen paused, collecting his thoughts. He'd waited five years to make this argument.

Speaking for half an hour, Ter Molen traced the long litany of Paula Gray's flip-flops before turning to the recent DNA results, which he said proved that Gray's original story had been fabricated.

"At this point, the evidence against Mr. Jimerson has been entirely negated," he said.

Ter Molen then addressed "the repeated misconduct by the state's attorney's office—an historical pattern going back to 1978 that entitles Mr. Jimerson to have the charges dismissed on the basis of due-process violations."

He cited, among other things, Scott Arthur's failure to correct Gray's perjury at Jimerson's trial and Clifford Johnson's "intentional misstatements" to Jimerson's grand jury about what Charles McCraney claimed to have seen.

Glancing at Zopp, Ter Molen concluded, "Indeed, with all due respect, dragging this out any longer would also be an example of misconduct."

Zopp rose in response, repeating that it was premature to dismiss the charges.

"Mr. Ter Molen says you can't believe anything that Paula Gray ever said. He might be right, but you have never seen her testify, so you don't know that."

Zopp called the allegations of misconduct "a huge leap to make. There is not one shred of evidence that prosecutors and police officers intentionally engaged in unethical conduct. I think we have a right to respond to that at a hearing."

"You've had an opportunity to respond for six months," Murphy interjected.

"I understand that," said Zopp. "But we have strong concerns about getting into a factual analysis at this time, and I know I am sort of doing doublespeak and I don't mean to be. What I'm trying to say to you is that we hope to have this matter resolved by early next week. . . . If you can let us get to July 2—"

"I denied that motion," said Murphy.

"I understand that, judge."

"About three times now."

Getting nowhere, Zopp concluded, "I still do not think you can reach the conclusion Mr. Ter Molen would like you to reach." Then she sat down.

Murphy cut right to the heart of the matter: "Taking the totality of the testimony before the trial court and also before the grand jury, it would be hard not to see that the circumstances here resulted in an egregious denial of due process to the defendant.

"If judges are meant to do anything, our duty is to hold up the law, the sky of our society.

"As we look at this entire case, it is clear that I have no choice but to grant your motion, Mr. Ter Molen.

"The indictment against Mr. Jimerson is hereby dismissed, and he is released from the custody of this court."

A rush of emotion swept the courtroom as Jimerson was mobbed by relatives screaming, "Praise the Lord!" and "Jesus, thank you!"

"You must maintain order," Murphy said.

The celebrants poured out of the courtroom, sweeping Jimerson along.

On the courthouse steps, his face smeared with lipstick, Jimerson told reporters he would move in with his brother and sister-in-law in Ford Heights, get a driver's license, and look for a job.

But first, he said, "I'm gonna visit my mother and father's graves."

TUESDAY, JULY 2, 1996

■ *8:30 A.M.*

Arthur "Red" Robinson gave it up.

Informed that DNA results had just come back showing that the semen on the swab and slide was his, Robinson confessed to raping and shooting Carol Schmal.

After waiving his right to counsel, he made the admissions during a court-reported interview at the state's attorney's office in the main Criminal Courts Building in Chicago.

"When we spoke on June fifteen, did you tell me all the details of your involvement in these crimes?" John Eannace asked.

"Some of it," Robinson responded. "I was scared."

"Can we talk further now about your involvement?"

"Yes."

"What did Dennis Johnson say once you got into the first floor of the townhouse?"

"He said, 'I'm gonna fuck the girl.' "

"After Dennis said that, what happened?"

"He did."

"Where did that occur?"

"Upstairs."

About ten minutes later, Robinson continued, Johnson came downstairs with Carol Schmal, who was crying and covering her breasts with her forearms.

"When Dennis brought the woman back downstairs, what happened?"

"Dennis gave me the .38 an' then we went upstairs, me an' the white girl."

"What did you tell her to do?"

"She took off her panties an' we had sex."

"After you had sex with her, what did the woman do?"

"She started cryin'. She asked me what was they gonna do to her.

"At that point, Johnson came back upstairs, and said, 'You're supposed to shoot her,' an' I said, 'No, I ain't gonna do it.' "Johnson then took the .38 and ordered her to perform oral sex, but she refused.

"Then what did Dennis say to her?"

" 'Bitch, I'm gonna shoot you.' He shot her dead center in the back of the head."

Then Johnson told Robinson, "Nigger, you're gonna shoot her, too."

"And when he told you that, Red, did Dennis give you the gun?"

"Yes."

"What did you do?"

"I turned my head an' shot."

"And when you say you shot, would that be at the woman on the floor?"

"Yes, yes."

Robinson, thereupon, was placed under arrest.

TUESDAY, JULY 2, 1996

■ *10:00 A.M.*

Twelve floors below, Dennis Williams, Kenny Adams, and Willie Rainge stood unbound before Judge Thomas Fitzgerald as Verneal Jimerson and more than a hundred other spectators looked on.

Fitzgerald read three documents the defense lawyers had prepared and, without objection, affixed his signature to each.

Then, he matter-of-factly ended an eighteen-year ordeal with five words: "All the convictions are vacated."

Standing motionless, the men waited for Fitzgerald to apologize or at least wish them well, but he was ready to move on to his next case.

The men turned, facing the spectators, who burst into a standing ovation.

Kenny Adams smiled shyly. Willie Rainge nodded appreciatively. And Dennis Williams returned the applause.

Their ankle bracelets were removed and they walked, with Jimerson, through the revolving door of the courthouse and into a perfect summer day.

■ ■ ■

The Ford Heights Four met the media on the courthouse steps.

Dennis Williams and Kenny Adams did the talking.

"Finally, officially, free!" Williams proclaimed, thrusting his fist into the air. "To put it bluntly, it's been pure hell."

"This is the type of day you dream about," said Adams. "I didn't think it was going to feel as good as it does.

"We are victims of this crime, too. I want people to know that this could happen to anybody—and that's a crime."

■ ■ ■

"You're ridin' with me," David Protess told Kenny Adams as the news conference broke up.

Adams didn't know it, but Protess had been planning the sojourn since seeing him at Danville three months earlier.

As Protess turned north from the Stevenson Expressway at McCormick Place, Lake Michigan came into view.

"Ohhhhh."

Adams pulled off his sunglasses.

"The colors. Blue—no, green. Ohhhhh. The sky, the sailboats. Look at that one!"

He lowered his window and breathed deeply. "I've missed this." Turning to Protess, he added, "I've missed a lot."

"So have I, Kenny," Protess replied. "So have I."

■ ■ ■

A few minutes later, David Protess and Kenny Adams arrived at the Fairmont Hotel, where channel 5 and NBCs *Dateline* were hosting a celebration for the men.

Protess and René Brown offered toasts, as an NBC cameraman and *People* magazine photographer captured the men tasting champagne for the first time in their lives.

When the students joined in the festivities, *People* snapped them with the men—in a pose reminiscent of the one that had gotten them banned from Illinois prisons.

Rob Warden arrived just as State's Attorney Jack O'Malley appeared on television to talk about the case. Warden had urged O'Malley to apologize, but didn't know if he'd follow the advice.

A hush fell over the party.

Said O'Malley: "Ours is the best system ever developed for administering justice, but it is not flawless. This case is a glaring example of its fallibility.

"I am sorry to these defendants personally and on behalf of the criminal justice system. I more than regret that there is not more I can do to undo the injustice. I cannot give these men those eighteen years back.

"When I say, 'I'm sorry,' I know those words are inadequate."

The men cheered.

"I never thought I'd ever see a prosecutor I'd like," said Dennis Williams.

Later that evening, the men had a decidedly different reaction to an appearance by Scott Arthur on *Dateline*.

Asked if he "would ever apologize," the prosecutor-that-was declared, "No—because I acted in good faith on everything that was brought to me."

WEDNESDAY, JULY 3, 1996

Eighteen years, one month, and twenty-three days after the slaying of Larry Lionberg and Carol Schmal, the state's attorney's office announced that it had, once again, solved the crime.

Ira Johnson, Arthur Robinson, and Juan Rodriguez were charged with two counts of first-degree murder each.

Reporters clamored for a reaction from the Ford Heights Four, who issued the following statement: "We hope the charges will bring a measure of justice to the victims' families. At the same time, we ask prosecutors not to compound a senseless tragedy by seeking the death penalty in any of these cases."

THURSDAY, JULY 4, 1996

As America celebrated Independence Day, scores of celebrants filled James and Vella Williams's backyard for a barbecue in honor of seven men who understood the true meaning of freedom.

There was James Newsome, about to enter law school after a stint as a paralegal at Jenner & Block, where he'd worked on Dennis Williams's case.

Newsome had been wrongly convicted of murder in 1981 and exonerated fourteen years later when new fingerprint tests proved he couldn't have committed the crime.

There was Delbert Tibbs, a published poet who counseled troubled youth at Hull House on Chicago's south side.

Tibbs had been wrongly convicted of murder in 1974 and exonerated eight years later when the lead prosecutor was forced to acknowledge that the evidence against him had been "tainted from the beginning."

And there was Darby Tillis, an ordained minister who preached the gospel on the streets and subways of the city.

Tillis had been wrongly convicted of murder in 1979, and exonerated eight years later when a prosecutor testified at his fifth trial that another person had confessed to the crime.

Like the Ford Heights Four, Newsome, Tibbs, and Tillis were African-Americans who'd been convicted of killing Caucasians. And they, too, had been doomed by false eyewitness testimony.

The Reverend Tillis, who'd befriended Dennis Williams and Girvies Davis on Death Row, welcomed the Ford Heights Four to a club they hadn't cared to join.

They were now among four hundred and twenty-one Americans in this century who'd been convicted of crimes punishable by death and later proven innocent. Twenty-three of these wrongly convicted Americans had been executed.

"We're the lucky ones," Tillis told Williams.

"Dead men talking," said Williams.

Looking to a night sky filled with fireworks, they prayed for the Preacherman, whose fate they'd been spared by God and man.

Epilogue

■ On April 28, 1997, after a four-day trial, Juan "Johnny" Rodriguez became the first person in Illinois history to be convicted of a murder for which someone else had been wrongly imprisoned.

The prosecution conceded there was no evidence that Rodriguez raped Carol Schmal or shot either victim, but argued that, under the law, he was just as culpable as those who did. "He was an accomplice, who acted in concert with the other three men," Assistant State's Attorney Alison Perona told the jury. "If you're in for the part, you're in for the whole."

Rodriguez took the stand, contending his participation in the crime had been coerced by the Johnson brothers. But the jury didn't buy it, deliberating less than three hours before finding him guilty.

When the verdict was read, Dennis Williams and Kenny Adams were in the front row of the courtroom, with Carol Schmal's family seated right behind them.

Carol's sister, Lynn, rested her arm on Adams's shoulder and said to both men, "I want you to know that we are truly sorry for what happened to you."

Williams replied, "We know your pain will never go away, but we hope you will find consolation in the truth."

■ ■ ■

Judge Daniel Kelley sentenced Juan Rodriguez to life in prison without the possibility of parole, saying Illinois law required nothing less in a multiple-murder case.

Within days, however, prosecutors discovered that Kelley had been wrong. In fact, the mandatory sentencing law he'd applied hadn't been in effect at the time of the crime.

So, after a hearing, Kelley resentenced Rodriguez to eighty years, meaning that his case would first be reviewed by a parole board in 2008.

Rodriguez appealed the conviction, claiming that his lawyer, Julie McBride, had been ineffective. At the time of the trial, she'd been facing disciplinary action for financial improprieties.

Shortly thereafter, she was suspended from the practice of law, a dishonor shared by three other defense lawyers in the Ford Heights case: Archie Weston, Isaiah "Skip" Gant, and Earl Taylor.

■ ■ ■

Prosecutors planned to seek the death penalty for Ira Johnson, who already stood convicted of the Cherry Wilder murder and had admitted killing Larry Lionberg.

Fulfilling a promise, David Protess cajoled one of Chicago's best-known criminal defense lawyers, Jack Rimland, to try to save Johnson's life.

Rimland in turn cajoled Andrea Zopp to offer Johnson life without parole in exchange for a guilty plea. But, if Johnson refused, the state would put him on trial and seek death.

On June 16, 1997, Johnson took the deal.

In an interview with Protess and Rob Warden at the Cook

County jail, Johnson said he'd reached his decision to plead guilty after praying daily with Sister Miriam Wilson, the jail chaplain who'd also counseled Verneal Jimerson.

Helping exonerate the innocent men, Johnson said, was the most honorable thing he'd done in his life, and he hoped it would help atone for "many terrible things."

When asked about the latter, he hesitated, finally saying, "I shared everything with Sister Miriam and with God. Let's just say I know about five other murders. Maybe my brother jus' told me about 'em, or maybe I was there."

He said all five murders were over drugs and, like Cherry Wilder's, occurred after the Schmal/Lionberg crime.

"I pray every day now for forgiveness," he said, "for my brother and for myself."

■ ■ ■

Having made a deal with Ira Johnson, prosecutors made the same offer to Arthur "Red" Robinson.

Robinson, who'd never been in prison, didn't relish the thought of being there for the rest of his life.

"Them prosecutors might as well kill me," he told David Protess in an interview at the county jail.

They decided to try.

But on the eve of trial, Robinson blinked, agreeing to plead guilty in order to escape the death penalty.

He was sentenced to life without parole on July 22, 1997.

"I got caught up in somethin' real bad and done an awful thing," he told Protess. "I ain't never hurt nobody before or since them two hours that night, an' now I'll be payin' for it forever.

"But you know somethin'? I done the right thing talkin' to y'all. My momma says she's proud of me for finally standin' up an tellin' the truth."

■ ■ ■

After an internal investigation, the Cook County Sheriff's Police deemed the conduct of its investigators perfectly proper.

Sgt. David Capelli denied that his notes of the Marvin Simpson interview—the street file—had been sanitized. According to Capelli, Simpson had said nothing about hearing shots or seeing Red Robinson and Ira Johnson run around the side of the abandoned townhouse.

Lt. Howard Vanick claimed he hadn't been present for the interview because he'd left Simpson's hospital room to make phone calls. Vanick's recollection, however, was that Simpson had named four men who had a history of robbing gas stations and had only speculated about their involvement in the Lionberg/Schmal crime.

Since the lead hadn't been specific, Vanick contended, he'd left it to George Nance to investigate and, after hearing nothing from Nance, assumed it hadn't panned out.

Sheriff Michael Sheehan accepted Capelli's and Vanick's explanations, and they remained on active duty at the sheriff's office.

"There does not appear to be any evidence of wrongdoing," Sheehan said through a spokesperson.

■ ■ ■

The Ford Heights Four considered the sheriff's investigation a whitewash.

In civil suits filed in 1997, seeking unspecified money damages, they accused David Capelli, Howard Vanick, and other investigators of "intentionally manufacturing false evidence" to convict them.

Dennis Williams, who was first to file, was represented by renowned Wyoming lawyer Gerry Spence, Verneal Jimerson by Mark Ter Molen, Willie Rainge by Lawrence Marshall and Matthew Kennelly, and Kenny Adams by Chicago lawyers Flint Taylor and Jeffrey

Haas, who'd represented George Jones in the 1982 murder trial that exposed street files.

Former assistant state's attorneys Scott Arthur, Clifford Johnson, and Deborah Dooling couldn't be sued because of the doctrine of sovereign immunity, which gives prosecutors broad protection from civil liability.

The Illinois Attorney Registration and Disciplinary Commission did open an investigation into prosecutorial misconduct soon after the supreme court ruled that prosecutors had failed to correct Paula Gray's perjury.

The commission, however, took no action against the prosecutors. That wasn't unusual. In the commission's thirty-four-year history, not a single prosecutor had been disbarred, or even suspended, for misconduct in a criminal case.

■ ■ ■

Following a federal investigation into Ford Heights police corruption, Chief Jack Davis and five other officers—more than half of the town's police department—were convicted in 1997 of extorting bribes from drug dealers and abetting them in the distribution of heroin and crack.

Drug dealers, in exchange for leniency, had carried hidden recorders to tape their meetings with Davis and the others. Among the dealers were Ira Johnson's sister and brother-in-law, April and Randolph Holmes.

Until replacements for Davis and the others could be recruited, the Cook County Sheriff's Department was assigned to patrol Ford Heights.

Interviewed by state's attorney's investigators, Davis said he recalled seeing George Nance's reports on the Lionberg/Schmal murder investigation, but they'd somehow disappeared.

The investigators didn't question Davis about his relationship to Sam and Marcella Johnson, or their children.

■ ■ ■

As Paula Gray struggled to resume a normal life, the Cook County Public Defender's Office assigned a new lawyer to her child-custody case. By sheer coincidence, the lawyer was Jeanne Bishop, who'd helped overturn Verneal Jimerson's conviction.

When Gray called to set up an appointment, Bishop was floored. "You're not *the* Paula Gray from the Ford Heights case, are you?"

"That don't got nothin' to do with this," Gray snapped.

Bishop explained her role in exposing Gray's perjury to the supreme court. "You might not want me as your lawyer," she said.

"I sure 'nuff do if you'll help me get my kids back."

After their first meeting a few days later, Bishop was taken by Gray's determination and sincerity.

Karma was at work, Bishop thought.

"There's no client I'm going to fight harder for than you," she promised.

Bishop arranged for Gray to get counseling and to enroll in parenting classes at a junior college near her home.

Gray's emotional strength grew, and she was punctual for every court hearing, even though she had to take four buses and a train each way.

But assistant state's attorneys, who'd obtained a court order to place the children in foster homes because of alleged abuse by their father, stiffened their will to terminate Gray's parental rights and put the children up for adoption.

Since the father had been out of the home for years, Bishop became convinced that the prosecutors' real agenda was to punish Gray for recanting to David Protess and his students.

The battle dragged on, and Gray began to lose hope.

Then an old boyfriend came to call.

"Paula, it's me, Kenny," said the voice on the intercom.

"Kenny? Kenny Adams?"

She felt a wave of fear and shame, which were quickly overcome by her longing to see him.

She buzzed him in.

When she opened the door, Kenny drew Paula to him and held her in his arms.

"Can you forgive me?" she whispered.

"I already did, a long time ago."

For an hour or so, they spoke of teenage dreams and innocence lost.

Paula proudly showed him photos of her four girls and two boys, and described her anguish over losing them.

"Th' prosecutors is beatin' me down, Kenny," she said.

"They did that before, but you finally beat 'em—an' you'll beat 'em again."

He told her to call him if she needed someone to lean on.

They would talk again, but he had already given her the resolve to continue the fight.

■ ■ ■

Carrying his only identification—a tattered birth certificate and his photo in *People* magazine—Kenny Adams tried to open a bank account with an $8,000 check he'd received as his share of the movie rights to the story of the Ford Heights Four.

"We require a photo ID with your signature on it," said a bank officer.

"But look, it's me," he said, pointing to the *People* photo.

"Sorry."

Another bank, same result.

In frustration, Adams turned to his congressman, Jesse Jackson, Jr.

The next day, the first bank sheepishly accepted Adams's deposit and welcomed him as a customer.

Adams faced greater hurdles finding a job.

Human resources departments wanted to know, among other things, his work history and whether he'd ever been convicted of a crime.

His fortunes finally turned after he mentioned in a television interview that he'd developed woodworking skills in prison.

A viewer called and offered two temporary job opportunities, building a trophy case for Wheaton High School and rehabbing an apartment building on Chicago's West Side.

Adams took them both, working seven days a week until the projects were finished.

Again unemployed, he turned to Congressman Jackson, who helped him land a part-time night job on a loading dock for a package-delivery service.

Arriving home from work one day, he found a letter from the Illinois State Police.

The letter informed him that he'd be arrested unless he promptly registered with his local police department—as a released sex offender.

This time, his criminal defense lawyer, Jeffrey Urdangen, intervened. The state police ultimately informed Adams he could disregard the letter, which had been "a paperwork mistake."

Undaunted by these indignities, Adams looked to the future, saving a few dollars from each paycheck to fulfill his dream of opening a woodworking shop.

And, a year after his release, he announced plans to marry. The bride-to-be was Norma Negron, a neighbor of James and Vella Williams. Norma and Kenny had met at the July 2, 1996, freedom party at the Fairmont Hotel. It had been love at first sight.

"All I ever wanted to do in life was to have a wife an' kids an' a good job," Kenny said, with Norma at his side. "It's been a long time comin', but I'm gettin' there."

■ ■ ■

Needing identification, Willie Rainge ordered his birth certificate from Sunflower County, Mississippi. When it came, he found out he wasn't who he thought he was.

Due to a thirty-nine-year-old typographical error, the document had incorrectly recorded his name as "Raines."

In no mood to butt heads with Mississippi bureaucrats, he opened a bank account and obtained a driver's license under the name on the birth certificate.

"I've been reborn," he joked.

William L. Raines spent part of his movie rights payment on a used conversion van, and headed to Ford Heights to show it off to family members.

He was waylaid.

Suburban police pulled him over, mistaking him for a long-wanted suspect in a string of burglaries.

It seemed a classic case of what defense lawyers call "DWB"—driving while black.

When the officers ran a computer check, they discovered that Raines was Rainge, and he had an air-tight alibi: He'd been in Stateville at the time of the crimes.

They wished him good luck and sent him on his way.

At the time, Rainge was spending his days caring for his son, Tederol, and his nights sleeping on Tederol's living room rug.

But the sleeping arrangement violated public housing rules—no two adults who aren't married are permitted to live in a one-bedroom apartment—and Rainge was soon threatened with eviction.

Facing homelessness, Rainge accepted the only job offer he'd received: a full-time maintenance job at a nursing home in Madison, Wisconsin. Within months, he was promoted to supervisor.

His daughter, Arealya, and her child moved in with him, and they were joined by Arealya's fiancé, Kenny Adams's brother, Timothy.

Meanwhile, Tederol entered a rehabilitation program at Northwestern University, where his condition improved and doctors predicted he would walk again.

Rainge had high hopes that Tederol would soon move to Madison, making the family whole.

■ ■ ■

Verneal Jimerson searched for solace at the Trinity Church of God, where he'd once been a choirboy.

The Reverend Charles Nelson, who'd been Jimerson's only witness at his 1985 death penalty hearing, officially welcomed him back to the fold at a July 27, 1996, memorial service for his parents.

In the first pew, Jimerson was flanked by Dennis Williams, Kenny Adams, and Willie Rainge, wearing white carnations in their lapels.

Among other honored guests were Marvin Simpson, George Nance, and René Brown, each of whom drew sustained applause.

The featured speaker was Jesse Jackson, Jr., who stirred the congregation with a speech in the style of his famous father.

"The Ford Heights Four are this community's greatest asset—an example for young people everywhere," he proclaimed. "You fought the good fight. You did the right thing. Don't let this experience make you bitter. Let it make you better."

Urging the congregation to open their "hearts and wallets" for the men, Jackson set an example by placing four $100 bills in a collection box for them.

Then a scarlet-robed women's choir sang:

I know somehow, and I know someday
We're gonna make it
No matter what comes our way, with Jesus on our side,
We're gonna make it.

Somehow, someday
*We're gonna make it.**

Outside after the ceremony, the village trustees announced that "Ford Heights Freedom Celebration Day" would be observed annually on July 27, and the four men released balloons the colors of kinte cloth into the overcast sky.

Jimerson told well-wishers he'd reestablished contact with his three daughters, who'd blessed him with five grandchildren, and with his ex-wife, who'd remarried a few years after the divorce he'd insisted on and now regretted.

He'd soon enroll in an auto-mechanics curriculum at a community college, under a scholarship arranged by Governor's State University President Paula Wolff.

The last time he'd worked on cars, they still had carburetors, plugs, and points. Now he had to learn about computer diagnostics, fuel injection, and antilock brakes.

Until he graduated, he'd get by on earnings from a part-time job at an auto detailing shop owned by the Reverend Nelson.

He'd spent most of his movie rights money on his offspring, hoping to make up for twelve Christmases missed.

■ ■ ■

On December 26, 1996, Verneal Jimerson was stopped by a Cook County Sheriff's Police officer for failing to signal before making a left turn from a parking lot in Chicago Heights.

The officer claimed to have noticed, "in clear view" on the seat beside Jimerson, a small plastic bag, the contents of which allegedly field-tested positive for marijuana and cocaine. Jimerson was ar-

*"We're Going to Make It" written by Timothy Wright. Copyright 1988 by Arisav Music, Inc. Used by permission. All rights reserved.

rested on the spot and charged with possession of a controlled substance.

On February 19, 1997, the case came before Markham Judge Will Gierach, the very judge who'd sentenced Jimerson to death twelve years earlier.

Rejecting the officer's contention that the bag had been in plain view, Gierach threw out the case for lack of probable cause to make the arrest, and Jimerson walked free.

Karma again.

■ ■ ■

Dennis Williams cashed his movie rights check at a bank after Jenner & Block associate Tamara Klein vouched that it was good.

Stuffing eighty crisp C-notes into his pants, Williams told Klein, "Anybody tries to take this away from me an' I'll be arrested for a crime I *did* commit."

He gave some to his family, bought art supplies, and made a down payment on his dream car, a 1997 black Mitsubishi Eclipse. Having no health insurance, he also paid for a battery of medical tests, which, to his relief, confirmed that he had no serious physical problems.

Near broke less than a month after his release, Williams filed a petition with the Illinois Court of Claims in 1997 under a statute that allows up to $140,000 compensation for wrongful incarceration.

Williams hesitated making the claim because the statute required him first to obtain a pardon from the governor, a step Williams thought perverse. The state, he felt, should be asking a pardon *from him*. Furthermore, he thought the amount was shameful: less than $8,000 a year for his time in prison. And, under the statute, he'd probably have to repay the money if he won the civil suit against the sheriff's police.

But Gerry Spence told him the civil suit could take years, and he had no income except a few hundred dollars from the occasional sale of a painting.

So Williams went forward, and on April 17, 1997, became the first condemned man in Illinois ever to receive a pardon based on innocence.

While awaiting the outcome of his legal claims, Williams took college preparatory courses and pursued his oil painting with a passion.

At an art fair where some of his works were exhibited, he found another passion—Eileen McCarthy, a social worker who lived in Oak Park, a block from the Protess family.

After a whirlwind courtship, Dennis moved in with Eileen, and they converted a spare bedroom into an art studio.

As Dennis celebrated his fortieth birthday, his first as a free man since he'd turned twenty-one, he made plans for a one-man show.

■ ■ ■

In July of 1997, Kenny Adams's sister, Juanita, hosted a black-tie dinner to celebrate the first anniversary of the release of the Ford Heights Four.

A surprise guest flew in from Los Angeles: Margaret Roberts, who'd moved on from *America's Most Wanted* to produce other television programs, including a talk show for the Reverend Jesse Jackson.

Dennis Williams didn't recognize her at first, having last seen her eleven years earlier as they sat on opposite sides of a Plexiglas barrier.

"Margaret, you look taller!" he exclaimed when Rob Warden reintroduced her.

They embraced, and she told him, "You look a lot different, too. You traded in your prison coveralls for a tuxedo."

"If it hadn't been for you," he replied, "I wouldn't ever have got dressed up again, 'cept maybe for my funeral."

They both smiled.

"Thank you," he said.

During dinner, Roberts was seated next to René Brown, whom she hadn't seen since 1982. They relived their sojourns to East Chicago Heights and their encounters with Dennis "the Dude" Johnson.

Brown told her that his more recent role in the case had inspired him to resume his career as a defense investigator. He'd just thrust himself into the case of an Illinois Death Row prisoner, Delbert Heard, who'd been convicted of a triple murder based almost solely on a dubious eyewitness account.

And David Protess made plans to hire him to work with Medill students on future investigations.

■ ■ ■

Dennis Williams and Kenny Adams resumed their close friendship and spent much of their free time speaking out on criminal justice issues.

They appeared on *Nightline*, *Good Morning America*, and Tom Snyder's *Late, Late Show*, among other programs.

But Williams insisted on doing the interviews remote from Chicago studios, having developed an intense fear of flying after Girvies Davis's helicopter trip to the death chamber.

Consumed by paranoia, Williams fantasized that, if he ever got on a plane, Scott Arthur somehow might have it blown up.

So when Congressman Jesse Jackson, Jr., asked him and Adams to testify in Washington about the public policy lessons of the case, Williams endured a nineteen-hour bus ride to get there.

The following day, Jackson introduced the men to a crowd of three hundred, including members of the Congressional Black Caucus, other legislators, congressional aides, reporters, and Jesse Jackson, Sr.

After Adams recounted the ordeal of the Ford Heights Four,

Williams rose to speak. He'd written countless legislators over the years about the case. None had listened, but they'd listen now.

He began by proposing five ways "to help restore justice to our criminal justice system": abolishing capital punishment, allowing petitions for new trials to be presented any time evidence of innocence is discovered (a right that had been severely curtailed by the Anti-Terrorism Act of 1996), repealing legislation intended to speed up capital appeals, raising the standards and reducing the caseloads of defense lawyers working at public expense, and ensuring every defendant's right to test possible DNA evidence.

"These changes are absolutely vital if you don't want to repeat what happened to us, and to many other victims of our system," he said.

"But it seems that a whole lot of people nowadays—they call themselves 'reformers'—want to cut back our legal rights when we need most to protect them.

"What motivates these pseudo reformers to promote injustice?

"I think it's fear. There's fear of crime, fear of different skin colors, fear of admitting mistakes.

"You got people here in the government who're so scared, and who represent people who're so scared, that they build more and more prisons while doing away with the safeguards that prevent them from being filled with innocent people. That's frightening to me.

"We can't go on being so scared of each other. We have to find a common ground, or else justice will be nothing more than just a promise—an empty promise."

Williams grew contemplative. "I've been afraid," he finally said, "and I guess you could say I used to be a racist, too. But it was mostly white folks who stepped up to help us.

"So there's one thing I learned for sure in eighteen years: If we can conquer our fears—whatever they are—there's *nothing* we can't do."

■ ■ ■

Southwest Airlines Flight 510 took off from Baltimore-Washington International Airport at 9:55 the next morning.

The multicolored Boeing 737 ascended into clouds above the Allegheny mountains, soared across Ohio and Indiana, and began its descent, banking north over Interstate 57 in Illinois.

One hour and forty-seven minutes after its departure, the plane touched down gently at Chicago's Midway Airport, delivering Kenny Adams, and Dennis Williams, safely home.

NOTES ON SOURCES

Although we didn't know it at the time, our research for this book began when Dennis Williams introduced himself to us—to Rob Warden in 1981, to David Protess in 1986.

Before beginning to write more than a decade later, we read the Cook County Sheriff's Police reports from the initial investigation, the grand jury and trial transcripts, the appellate court opinions, and the interviews conducted by state's attorney's investigators with and about the alternate suspects. One or both of us was present at every significant court hearing in 1996 and 1997.

Most of the quotations that appear in the book are verbatim from the official record or tape-recorded interviews, although we occasionally have made alterations for intelligibility.

The dialogue that isn't in the public record, or that we didn't hear ourselves, has been reconstructed from the memories of the participants. We also relied on our own contemporaneous notes and, among others, those of Margaret Roberts, René Brown, and the students who worked on the case.

Occasionally, for the sake of the narrative, we have presented events slightly out of chronological sequence. When a date is stated, however, it is the actual date of the event.

After signing a contract to write this book in August of 1996, Warden resigned from the state's attorney's office, but continued his close association with Jack O'Malley. (Warden served as issues director for O'Malley's reelection campaign until November, when O'Malley lost his bid for a third term to Democrat Richard Devine.) Protess took a leave of absence from Northwestern University in December of 1996. We worked full-time on the book through the following summer.

In the course of our research and writing, we found these books about miscarriages of justice to be informative:

Adams, Randall. *Adams vs. Texas.* New York: St. Martin's Press, 1991.

Borchard, Edwin M. *Convicting the Innocent.* New Haven, Conn.: Yale University Press, 1932.

Brandon, Ruth and Christie Davies. *Wrongful Imprisonment: Mistaken Convictions and Their Consequences.* Hamden, Conn.: Archon Books, 1973.

Carter, Dan T. *Scottsboro: A Tragedy of the American South.* Baton Rouge, La.: Louisiana State University Press, 1979.

Carter, Rubin. *Sixteenth Round.* Toronto: Viking, 1974.

Conlon, Gerry. *In the Name of the Father.* New York: Plume, 1993.

Connery, Donald S. *Guilty Until Proven Innocent.* New York: G.P. Putnam's Sons, 1977.

Dinnerstein, Leonard. *The Leo Frank Case.* Athens: University of Georgia Press, 1987.

Ganey, Terry. *St. Joseph's Children.* New York: Lyle Stuart, 1989.

Gardner, Erle Stanley. *The Court of Last Resort.* New York: William Morrow & Co., 1952.

Hale, Leslie. *Hanged in Error.* Baltimore: Penguin Books, 1961.

Haresign, Gordon. *Innocence.* Grand Rapids, Mich.: Zondervan Books, 1986.

Kennedy, Dolores. *William Heirens: His Day in Court.* Chicago: Bonus Books, 1991.

Kennedy, Ludovic H. *The Airman and the Carpenter.* New York: Viking, 1986.

Lassers, Willard J. *Scapegoat Justice.* Bloomington, Ind.: Indiana University Press, 1973.

Radelet, Michael L. et al. *In Spite of Innocence: Erroneous Convictions in Capital Cases.* Boston: Northeastern University Press, 1992. (This book was the basis for Rev. Darby Tillis's assertion, reported in Chapter 16, that 421 Americans have been wrongly convicted of offenses punishable by death in this century.)

Radin, Edward D. *The Innocents.* New York: William Morrow & Co., 1964.

Tucker, John C. *May God Have Mercy.* New York: W. W. Norton, 1997.

Vogel, Steve. *Reasonable Doubt.* Chicago: Contemporary Books, 1989.

Yant, Martin. *Presumed Guilty.* Buffalo, N.Y.: Prometheus Books, 1991.

Young, Norman H. *Innocence Regained: The Fight to Free Lindy Chamberlain.* Annandale, Queensland, Australia: Federation Press, 1989.

For further information about persons wrongly sentenced to death in Illinois, see the MacArthur Justice Center's Internet site: www.ninelives.org.

■ ■ ■

For discussions of the culture of Death Row, we found two books particularly illuminating:

Prejean, Helen. *Dead Man Walking.* New York: Random House, 1993.

Von Drehle, David. *Among the Lowest of the Dead.* New York: Times Books, 1995.

■ ■ ■

A note about financial matters: The Ford Heights Four agreed to cooperate fully without remuneration. However, because they were in dire need, we subsequently decided to split equally among them the portion of our book proceeds that we didn't require for living expenses during the nine months we spent writing the book. As mentioned in the epilogue, the men also received payments for a possible movie about their case.

ACKNOWLEDGMENTS

We are deeply indebted to:

Our wives, Joan Protess and Jennifer Alter Warden, and our eldest sons, Daniel Protess and Rollins Warden, who provided constant encouragement and invaluable advice on our continually evolving manuscript.

Four friends—Alex Kotlowitz, Grace Mark, Brian Ross, and James Tuohy—who offered creative suggestions about organization and style.

The Ford Heights Four, their families, and Paula Gray, all of whom cooperated fully at every stage of our research and tolerated our frequent intrusions upon their privacy. (Dennis Williams also provided his file of correspondence spanning his years of incarceration.)

Carol Schmal's sister, Lynn Fisher, three of Carol's friends, Jane Adducci, Marlene Majka, and Rita Ward, and two of Larry Lionberg's friends, Charles and Donald Davidson, all of whom shared both painful and joyous memories.

Investigators René Brown and Paul Ciolino, whose friendship we treasure and whose dedication to justice continues to inspire us.

Lawyers who generously shared their time and insights: Jeanne Bishop, Barbara Blaine, Locke Bowman, Robert Byman, Martin Carlson, Thomas Decker, Charles Glick, Jeffrey Haas, Kendall Hill, Russell Hoover, William H. Jones, Matthew Kennelly, Peter M. King, Tamara Klein, Norbert Knapke, Barry Levenstam, Andrea Lyon, Lawrence Marshall, Julie McBride, Thomas Peters, Jack Rimland, Gerry Spence, Mark Ter Molen, Barry Scheck, David Schwartz, Flint Taylor, James L. Thompson, Jeffrey Urdangen, and Theodore Williams. And paralegals Sharon Klaber, James Newsome, and Wayne Stemmer.

Other lawyers who facilitated our interviews with the actual perpetrators of the crime: Kimball Anderson, Bruce Braun, and Raymond Perkins, for Arthur "Red" Robinson; Jack Rimland, for Ira Johnson; and Richard J. O'Brien and John Gallo, for Juan "Johnny" Rodriguez.

Judges who graciously consented to interviews: Seymour Simon, Sheila Murphy, and Reginald Baker.

Former State's Attorney Jack O'Malley and First Assistant Andrea Zopp, who provided behind-the-scenes details, and their spokespersons, Andy Knott, Marcy O'Boyle, and Timothy Touhy.

Present and former residents of Ford Heights—David Campbell, Annie Coulter, Naomi Elizondo, Emir Hardy, Patricia Hatten, George Nance, the Reverend Charles Nelson, Curt and Dorothy Robinson, Marvin Simpson, and Marian Walk—who raised the curtain on a community that outsiders rarely see.

Anti-death-penalty crusader Clarence Archer, who provided helpful insights and first coined the phrase "The Ford Heights Four."

Journalists Marsha Bartel, Tracy Haynes, Doug Longhini, Larry Potash, Dave Savini, Don Terry, Crystal Yednak, and Eric Zorn, whose commitment was unflagging and whose camaraderie we enjoyed. And Ken Armstrong, who checked the manuscript for factual accuracy.

Former students at Northwestern University's Medill School of Journalism, including Alexis Chiu, Cynthia Johnson, Alex Kuli, Wendy Raney, Jennifer Scroggins, and Lori Suderman, who provided valuable research, and Lara Flint, Deepti Hajela, Rainy Monson, Ryan Owens, Carrie Rabin, Stacey Rosenberg, Greg Shea, Sarah Wyatt, Crystal Yednak, and Su-jin Yim, who selflessly dedicated themselves to Girvies Davis's cause. And, of course, Stacey Delo, Stephanie Goldstein, Christe Guidibaldi, and Laura Sullivan.

Illinois Department of Corrections spokesperson Nic Howell, who arranged interviews at the Danville, Menard, Pontiac, and Stateville prisons.

Professor Abe Peck, former acting dean of Medill, and Professor Fay Cook, director of Northwestern's Institute for Policy Research, whose support made this project possible.

Jan Boudart, of the Medill support staff, who made our lives a lot easier.

Molly Friedrich, Kris Dahl, and Jeanne Williams, agents extraordinaire.

Finally, Brian DeFiore and Leigh Haber, our editors, and John Freeman, Haber's able assistant, who believed in the project and brought it to fruition.

INDEX